REFLECTIONS ON THE GOSPELS

by

Dr. Vance Havner

Written during the 1930s
Previously unpublished in book form

Compiled by
Michael C. Catt

Copyright © 2003 by Michael C. Catt

Reflections on the Gospels
by Michael C. Catt

Printed in the United States of America

Library of Congress Control Number: 2003102309
ISBN 1-591606-27-6

All rights reserved. No part of this publication may be reproduced, stored in a retrieval system, or transmitted in any form or by any means–electronic, mechanical, photocopy, recording, or any other–except for brief quotations in printed reviews, without the prior permission of the publisher.

Scripture quotations in this publication are from the *King James Version of the Bible*, unless otherwise identified.

For additional copies or more information on materials by Vance Havner, contact:

Sherwood Communications Group
2201 Whispering Pines Rd.
Albany, GA 31707
or
www.VanceHavner.com

Reprinted with permission from *The Charlotte Observer*. Copyright owned by *The Charlotte Observer*.

Xulon Press
10640 Main Street
Suite 204
Fairfax, VA 22030
(703) 934-4411
XulonPress.com

To order additional copies, call 1-866-909-BOOK (2665).

CONTENTS

Part One – Reflections on the Gospel of Matthew 15
- The Gospel According to You 17
- Why the Genealogies? 19
- Thou Shalt Call His Name Jesus 21
- The Hidden Years 23
- Divine Healing 25
- The Beatitudes 27
- The Law and the Prophets 29
- Good-For-Nothing Christians 31
- Faith and Care 33
- When Thou Prayest 37
- How Are You Building? 39
- Faith and Fear 41
- The Healer 45
- As Thou Hast Believed 47
- March 19, 1939 49
- The Gadarene 51
- According to Your Faith 53
- New Wine in Old Bottles 55
- Dawn From the Mountain 57
- According to Your Faith 59
- Twelve Sent Forth 61
- Warnings and Invitations 63
- Three Kinds of Burdens 65
- The Sower 69
- Not Law But Love 71
- An Enemy Hath Done This 73
- The Kingdom in Parable 75
- Faith and Doubt 77
- Walking the Waves Toward Jesus 81
- Walking the Waves to Jesus 85

- Give Ye Them to Eat 87
- Keep Thy Heart 89
- As Thou Wilt 91
- Why Reason Ye? 93
- Faith and Spiritual Stupidity 95
- Thou Art the Christ 99
- This is My Beloved Son 101
- As a Little Child 103
- The Unmerciful Servant 105
- Occupy Till I Come 107
- By What Authority 109
- What Think Ye of Christ? 111
- The Last Supper 113
- Where Are You at Calvary? 115
- He is Risen 117
- Our Marching Orders 121
- The Keys of Christ 125

Part Two – **Reflections on the Gospel of Mark** 127
- A Prophet in His Own Country 129
- Follow Me 131
- The Fever Cure 133
- Lord of the Sabbath 135
- The Unpardonable Sin 137
- The Family of the Spirit 141
- What Manner of Man! 143
- Only Believe 145
- One Thing Thou Lackest 147
- The Faith of God 149
- Almost to Jesus 151
- The Divine Paradox 153
- Out to See Jesus 157

Part Three – **Reflections on the Gospel of Luke** 159
- Thy Prayer is Heard 161

Contents

- Blessed Among Women 163
- No Room For Jesus 165
- Tempted Like As We 167
- Lepers are Cleansed, the Lame Walk 169
- As Thou Hast Believed 171
- The Raising of Lazarus 173
- The Blessing of the Unoffended 175
- For She Loved Much 177
- Three Gospel Snapshots 179
- Three Gospel Snapshots 183
- The 70 and the Samaritan 185
- Nothing to Set Before Him 187
- Denouncing the Pharisees 189
- Thou Fool, This Night 191
- Except Ye Repent 193
- February 19, 1939 195
- I and My Father Are One 197
- When a Man Comes to Himself 199
- Make Friends With Money 201
- If They Hear Not Moses 203
- No Joy Allowed 205
- Christ the Opener 207
- February 26, 1939 211

Part Four – Reflections on the Gospel of John 213
- A New Life Begun 215
- Come and See 217
- Three "Musts" of John 3 219
- John 3:16 221
- Condemned 223
- The Increasing Christ 225
- At Jacob's Well 229
- At Jacob's Well 231
- Go Thy Way 233
- At the Pool of Bethesda 235

- Wilt Thou Be made Whole? 237
- I Am the Life 239
- At the Feast 241
- Go and Sin No More 243
- Let Your Light So Shine 245
- The Light of the World 247
- The Good Shepherd 249
- Christ the Door 251
- The Raising of Lazarus 253
- The Farewell Discourse 255
- Constantly Abiding 257

FOREWORD

I miss Vance Havner. It seems like he was around all of my life.

When I was a seminary student in Chicago, he spoke in chapel, and I still remember the introduction: "Some of you men are more concerned about your dispensations than you are your dispositions." I also remember an outline he dropped into the message, based on Hebrews 11: "Moses saw the invisible, chose the imperishable and did the impossible." It's hard not to steal that one!

As a young pastor in the greater Chicago area, I often heard him preach over WMBI, the Moody Bible Institute radio station, either from the Winona Lake (Indiana) Bible Conference or Founder's Week at the Institute. There was always a freshness about each message, solid Bible truth blended with common sense and subtle humor. He is still the most quotable preacher I have ever heard, and I quote him often.

In later years, sometimes we'd find ourselves speaking at the same conference and we'd usually take time to chat. He always had a new story to tell or he'd ask me about my ministry and what the Lord was saying to me. He knew more about the ministry than I did, so I just let him talk while I drank it in. Just being with him was a benediction.

Very early in my ministry I learned to appreciate his

books and began to collect them. You can read his messages over and over and get something new from them each time. I'm glad that some of his books are being reprinted and that some newly discovered material is being published for the first time. The new generation of preachers needs to get acquainted with this homiletical giant and learn from him. His messages are as relevant today as when he first preached them.

I miss him. I look forward to seeing him again. Meanwhile, I'm grateful for his books. I can hear his voice in every line, and what he says still does me good. It will do you good, too.

Warren W. Wiersbe

Dedicated to the memory of

RON DUNN

Expositor, author, conference speaker, advisor, hero in the faith, overcomer, wise sage, quick wit, and dearest friend.

Vance Havner loved Ron Dunn. He wrote the foreward to one of Ron's books. He called Ron, "one of America's great up and coming preachers" – he was.

INTRODUCTION

I first met Vance Havner when he came to my home church in Mississippi to preach a revival. Although I was a teenager, the old preacher impacted my life in ways that are impossible to put down in the limited space afforded me in an introduction. Suffice it to say, during the formative years of my ministry, personal time and correspondence over the course of fifteen years, Havner impacted my philosophy of ministry.

Vance Havner, in many ways, was the last prophet of the 20th century. Prophets are a rare breed and an endangered species. Vance Havner was never afraid to say, "Thus saith the Lord..." and let the chips fall where they may. He had a keen insight, a blend of godly wisdom, mountain humor and old fashioned values that appealed to young and old alike.

In the 1980s, my wife and I traveled to Charlotte, North Carolina and spent several days searching through the archives of the *Charlotte Observer* for "Havner's Reflections" – articles written by Dr. Havner in the 1930s. The articles that appear in this book are the result of that search. This book is long overdue. To my knowledge, these articles have never appeared in this form in any other book by Dr. Havner. Having every book he ever published, I believe this is the first time they have appeared, in their original form, since they were published over 70 years ago as a weekly column. I have chosen to make no editorial changes, so you can catch the flavor of the man. These articles were selected because they are each built around Dr. Havner's reflections on the Gospels.

I hope you will enjoy reading these timeless reflections as much as I have enjoyed putting them together. If they bless your life, pause and pray that God will raise up another Havner, who will take the prophet's mantle and proclaim the Word – even if it costs him his head.

I am indebted to Dr. Warren Wiersbe, the late Ron Dunn and the late Lehman Strauss who have encouraged me. Their love for Vance Havner was the common ground that brought us together. The stories shared about this dear man of God allowed us to cross generational gaps and develop a fellowship that is only for the heavenly minded. It is my prayer, that the words and the man will bless your life. He certainly blessed ours.

Michael C. Catt
Albany, Georgia
December, 2002
www.vancehavner.com

PART ONE

REFLECTIONS ON THE GOSPEL OF MATTHEW

"The Gospel According to You"
September 8, 1929

Matthew, Mark, Luke and John are not the only Gospels. There is the Gospel according to You.

Most people do not read the Four Gospels. Once in a while they hear a few verses in a sermon. Or read a chapter for conscience's sake. Or listen to a message in Sunday school or at a funeral. But for the most part the first Gospels lie untouched. A diamond mine on the library table explored, while we chase dirt and dollars!

But people will read the Gospel according to You. For if you are one of His disciples, you are a living "epistle, known and read of all men." The life you live is His personal witness and it will be read and studied where the other Gospels lie unused.

Men do not read the beatitudes. But if you are poor in spirit, if you are meek and hungering for righteousness, if you are a peacemaker, pure in heart, they will not be slow to see it and call you blessed.

They may not study the Master's life nor follow Him in His gracious ministry along the roads of Galilee. But if you go about doing good, speaking love and truth, radiant with His Spirit, they will be reading in you the Gospel after all.

They may not know the parables nor delight in the beautiful imagery with which He painted the pictures of His

Kingdom but if you walk in the light as He is in the Light you will be a living human symbol of His grace and truth.

What sort of Gospel is this Gospel according to You? Is it a whole Gospel, a full reflection of the original? Or, is it a partial and patchy Gospel made of verses snatched from here and there, just these passages that suit your whims and fancies?

Some of these human gospels compare rather badly with Matthew, Mark, Luke and John. They come out strongly enough on these sections that happen to coincide with their pet, private notions. But they shine weakly or not at all where some personal sacrifice is required.

We have known some that talked a great deal about the wedding at Cana where there was plenty of wine. And skipped altogether that passage about "offending one of these little ones" with its subsequent advice to pluck out whatever offends. Such Gospels are man-made parodies on the true and misrepresentations.

But the living Gospel that goes abut reliving the Master here and now—what a beautiful Gospel is that! It is easily readable, truly practical and breathes not the breath of libraries, but of life. It translates the ideal into the actual, the theory into practice, and by it once again the Word becomes flesh and dwells among us.

And the Master Himself, who is really the Gospel, thought highly of these editions when He declared that not those who only prophesied in His Name should be accepted at the Great Day, but rather those whose daily ministrations of love and kindness proclaimed more truly than any book they could write their loyalty to Him. Above hymn and book and sermon He values the Gospel according to You.

"Why the Genealogies?"
January 13, 1935

The long list of our Lord's ancestry given in Mt. 1:1-17 and Lk. 3:23-38 have puzzled the devout not a little. They are not identical and the ordinary reader wades through the formidable catalogues perhaps to no great edification.

But there is a definite purpose and value to every portion of the God-breathed Scriptures. Matthew, writing to Jews, traces our Lord on His human side back to Abraham. Luke, writing to gentiles, goes back to Adam. Matthew traces the line to David through our Lord's legal father, Joseph. Notice the changed expression in 1:16: "Joseph the husband of Mary, of whom was born Jesus, who is called Christ." Matthew, representing Christ the King, gives His kingly descent.

Much difficulty attend the fact that Jacob is given as Joseph's father in Matthew while Luke says "Joseph which was of Heli" (3:23.) It is believed that in Luke we have the ancestry of Mary whose father was Heli, therefore Joseph as son-in-law is called son.

Whatever the explanation of that, the lists afford us spiritual meat. Our Lord is the heir by descent to the throne of David which throne He will yet occupy when He reigns on earth over a redeemed Israel.

All classes occur in this line, good and bad, rich and poor. Our Lord is the representative of collective humanity. All of us may find our types in this line of descent. He was identified in His ancestry with all sorts. Three women who were guilty of gross sins are found here, Rahab, Tamar and Bathsheba. On our side, the Lord Jesus inherited all the common tendencies of humanity that He might be tempted in all points like as we. Yet He was without sin.

On the human side He comes though all this checkered ancestry, truly representative of the race, Jew and Gentile blood in His veins. On the divine side He comes from God, the express image of God, the Word, Emmanuel. These are joined in the supreme miracle of all time, Jesus Christ the God-man.

So legally through Joseph and actually through Mary our Lord is linked with David and Abraham in the Gospel to the Jews and with Adam in the Gospel to the Gentiles. And both writers are careful to declare His virgin birth. Matthew with his "Joseph the husband of Mary, of whom was born Jesus, who is called Christ" and Luke with "Jesus...being (as we supposed) the son of Joseph."

Familiarity with the story has dulled us to the wonder and mystery of this marvel of all time, God becoming man. How carefully the stage is set, the Roman, Jew and Greek worlds converging on this focal point, each with its own contribution! And God maintained through the centuries the line of descent until the fullness of time He should send forth His son born of a woman.

No page of His record is dull when seen in the light of His wonderful purpose!

"Thou Shalt Call His Name Jesus"
February 3, 1935

Only Matthew and Luke give us any account of the birth of our Lord. Matthew records that Mary "was found with child of the Holy Ghost" and that the angel appearing to Joseph declares the child shall be called Jesus, which is equivalent to the Old Testament Joshua and means Saviour. All this also is a fulfillment of Isa. 7:14.

Luke records more details. Joseph and Mary at Bethlehem for the taxation find no room in the inn. Alas, there still is no room for the Lord Jesus to be born in the crowded inns of many hearts.

The Lord Jesus was first made known to shepherds who represent the working class; to the wise men, who represent the student class; and to Simeon and Anna, who represent the worshiping class. Christ has ever been made known to men in their work, their study, their worship. It is significant that the first to hear the glad tidings were the humble shepherds, as if to declare in advance that these things should be received by the weak and base and despised, more by babes than by the wise and prudent.

Yet the learned are not excluded for the wise men also came to the young King. This story has been twisted somewhat out of its original shape. It is not said that there were three, nor are their names given. Their gifts are significant:

gold symbolizes royalty; frankincense speaks of the fragrance of our Lord's life, sacrifice to the Father; myrrh, used in embalming the dead, point to His death. In Isa. 60:6 similar gifts are spoken of in connection with our Lord's Return but the myrrh is omitted for His death then is past.

In Matthew's account several Scriptures are fulfilled. Micah 5:2 in regard to Bethlehem comes to pass. The flight to Egypt fulfills Hosea 11:1 which applies primarily to Israel but also to our Lord who was identified with His brethren according to the flesh. Jer. 31:15 is fulfilled in the laughter of the children by Herod. It personifies Israel in Rachel weeping for her children. The contest shows that Israel will weep until she accepts her Messiah.

Mary must offer sacrifice (Lk. 2:24) because she was sinful as other women. Devout Simeon and Anna waiting for the consolation of Israel and not to die until they had seen the Christ are Spirit-led to recognize Him. Simeon quotes from Isa. 42 and 8 that the Lord Jesus shall be a light to the Gentiles, the glory of Israel and a stumbling stone to Israel (Rom. 3:92; 1 Cor. 1:23, 24; 2 Cor. 2:16; 1 Pt. 2:7.) Truly a sword pierced Mary's heart at the cross (Jn. 19:25) as Simeon declared. The rest of the verse, "that the thoughts of many hearts may be revealed" belongs to verse 34. In the attitude men take toward Christ all else is revealed.

Anna testified to others who looked for the Messiah, but doubtless her witness to other Jews was rejected as it has been to this day.

"The Hidden Years"
February 10, 1935

Matthew covers our Lord's childhood and youth with one rich sentence (2:23): "And He came and dwelt in a city called Nazareth; that it might be fulfilled which was spoken by the prophets, He shall be called a Nazarene."

This prophecy undoubtedly involves a play on the word "netzer" or "rod" of Isa. 11:1. It is good to know that our Lord was content to grow up in a humdrum and despised village from whence nothing good was expected (Jn. 1:46). He knew the daily grind of the commonplace and the problems of the common people. No wonder they heard Him gladly.

Luke goes more into detail and gives us one rich incident from these hidden years in Chapter 2:40-52. This account begins and ends with verses, which form a beautiful frame for the picture: "And the child grew and waxed strong in spirit, filled with wisdom: and the grace of God was upon him." "And Jesus increased in wisdom and stature and in favor with God and man." Thus His complete development, physical, mental, spiritual and social, is declared.

Many questions arise concerning these silent years. Thirty years of simple living, next to nature and amidst humanity and busy at work with time to read and pray–it is a life this feverish age does not know. It shows its flavor in the many references to sparrow, lilies, the sower, the fields; it is colored with the atmosphere of the field, the fisherman's boat and net, the sea, the shop, the soil. If we had planned the life of the Son of God we would have put Him through universities, made Him a world traveler, put Him into society, places of earthly position and power. Never would we have selected thirty years at Nazareth as the ideal course! Truly His ways are not ours!

The solitary incident in the Temple reveals that He knew Who His real Father was and what His own work was. Mary tells Him: "Thy father and I have sought thee sorrowing." He replies: "Wish ye not that I must be about my Father's business?" He knew His true Father and His primary obligation. That they understood not what He spake shows that He referred to His life work as Messiah and Saviour, and not merely to worship, which they would have understood.

But immediately follows what appeals more to me than His wisdom in the temple. You and I might have grown vain over our success in the temple but the Son of God is willing to go back to the shop at Nazareth for many more years of its daily grind. To me He is even greater turning back toward Nazareth than in the temple.

Notice, too, how the Holy Spirit guards against any inference that He repudiated parental authority by what He said about His Father's business, "He was subject unto them." No boy prodigy would have turned from such glory as Jerusalem to the grind at Nazareth.

The hidden years at Nazareth carry rich lessons for us. If we would truly be of the sect of the Nazarenes (Acts 24:5) we would do well to get into our lives more of the simplicity, the patience, the willingness to tread the common path, the quiet waiting of the Nazarene.

"Divine Healing"
November 4, 1934

The very words are misleading as though all healing were not the work of God. But of direct healing without any intermediate agencies we hear much today and that usually is called Divine healing.

Our Lord's ministry upon earth was one of preaching, teaching and healing (Mt. 4:23). Power to heal was to be a sign of believers (Mk. 16:18.) The apostles healed (Acts 3:1-11; 9:32-43; 14:8-10.) Healing is listed as one of the spiritual gifts (1 Cor. 12:9.) James declares that the prayer of faith shall save the sick (Jas. 5:15.)

That God heals today in direct answer to prayer is proven again and again in undeniable instances some of which all of us have known. In other cases He heals through the agencies of doctors and medicines. In other cases where healing is asked just as earnestly for some reason best known to Himself He does not heal at all. There is no uniform rule here that fits all cases.

Paul healed yet he himself carried a "thorn in the flesh" which God did not take away in answer to prayer. He left Trophimus at Miletum sick (2 Tim. 4:20) and he advised Timothy to use a little wine for his stomach's sake and his often infirmities (1 Tim. 5:23).

These facts, with the facts of everyday experience, bear

out the truth that God is not always pleased to heal the sick even in answer to earnest prayer. The "prayer of faith" that shall save the sick is prayer that is in line with God's will to heal in a given case. The true attitude of faith is "Thy will be done" and when it is God's will to heal in a certain case and the prayer is in harmony with His will it is a true prayer of faith.

It is the same principle where we read that if we delight ourselves in the Lord He shall give us the desires of our hearts (Ps. 37:4.) One readily can see how that if every one got from God what he desired we should have hopeless confusion with two men, for instance, in the same community praying, one for rain and the other for dry weather. The antecedent conditions that we delight in the Lord, rest in His will, and then the desire or our hearts will be that His will be done. In other words, as we abide in Him He creates within us such holy desires as He is pleased to answer.

The true attitude toward healing is to trust one's condition with the Lord, commit it to Him at the outset. Then, it is well to use such agencies as we can for healing and recovery for they, too, are the gifts of God. Committing one's case to a doctor does not exclude the participation of God for whatever good results are obtained come from the giver of every good and perfect gift. God often uses means as He did with the poultice of figs in Hezekiah's case (Isa. 38:21) and as our Lord did with the blind man (John 9:6). Still, He can and often does heal when all earthly means have failed so our attitude should be that God does heal and sometimes uses means rather than that nature heals us with the aid of medicine and sometimes God may heal. One attitude puts the possibility of Divine Healing.

"The Beatitudes"
June 23, 1935

The sermon on the mount has been twisted to suit more divergent views than any other portion of our Lord's message. Some have made it the summary of His teaching as though He said nothing else while others have transferred it over into a future age with a purely Jewish application as though it meant nothing for us today. It is true that his message has Israel primarily in mind and its literal fulfilment will be in the kingdom age to come when Christ rules over Israel but it has a personal spiritual application for us now.

The well-known beatitudes set forth the characteristics of the citizens of His kingdom and we who believe today should bear these marks of the mount. The poor in spirit are those who know themselves to be nothing and that their only sufficiency is in Him. They are not necessarily the poor in pocketbook though, doubtless, most of the poor in spirit are poor in purse. To be poor in one's own spirit should be the counterpart to being rich in His Spirit, "having nothing, yet possessing all things."

The mournful are not merely those who mourn, in trouble but rather those who lament their own spiritual weakness and poverty, whose cry is, "Woe is me, for I am undone." Such tears precede great blessing unless one wallows in self-pity and gets no further.

The meek are the lowly and gentle, not milksops and dish-rag characters as some think. These shall inherit the earth in spite of those who say the only way they could ever get it would be to inherit it. It is the Lamb Who finally prevails.

To hunger and thirst after righteousness is a lost experience with most professing Christians who are too shallow and superficial or else too fed-up with the lollipops of earth really to crave deeper blessing. A deep spiritual feast must follow a deep hunger and a big appetite!

The merciful are those who are long-suffering toward others, considerate of human weakness, full of love which "suffereth long and is kind." The pure in heart are those who follow holiness without which no man shall see the Lord. If the heart be pure, there will be no trouble with the conduct for out of the heart are the issues of life.

The peacemakers are not merely those who arbitrate and settle quarrels, although that is included, but those whose spirit creates an atmosphere of peace. Having peace with God and the peace of God they make for peace wherever they go.

Few are the persecuted and reviled today for His sake. And, mind you, we are blessed only when we are evil spoken against falsely for His sake. "Falsely for His sake" brings in two important qualifications.

Christians are the salt of the earth, purifying, preserving, creating a thirst for the Water of Life. They keep the earth from putrefaction as will be proven when the church is removed. When it is without savor, an empty profession, it is trodden under foot in contempt. We are also the light of the world (Phil. 2:15) even as He is the Light of the world (John 8:12) and our business is not to shine our light but simply to let it shine that others seeing may glorify, not us but our Heavenly Father.

"The Law and the Prophets"
June 30, 1935

Our Lord's relation to the Mosaic Law has been misunderstood grievously. He declared that He came not to destroy the law but to fulfill it (Mt. 5:17) and that is the key to the whole matter. Some speak slightly of the law as though our Lord roughly disannulled it but He regarded it as sacred. The Law was the bud and He the blossom fulfilling it but both bud and blossom are perfect in their own way.

The law is "holy, just and good" but believers are not under law but under grace and inlawed to Christ, "married to another" (Rom. 7:4). Christ was born under the law (Gal. 4:4), lived under the law, kept the law perfectly, bore the curse of the law in His death and thereby redeemed us from it that we might be dead to it and bear fruit unto God (Rom. 7:4).

In the sermon on the mount our Lord set forth His relation to the law and the prophets. Far from disregarding the law He declared that every jot and tittle should be fulfilled. Our righteousness must exceed the law-righteousness of the Pharisees and it does because Christ Himself is our righteousness (2 Cor. 5:21; 1 Cor. 1:30.)

Then our Lord went back of the law to show that the real offence lay in the evil motive, the cause of sin. He showed that murder went back to hatred and anger, adultery to lust. He then laid down the only reason for divorce, fornication.

Frivolous swearing and serious oaths alike are set aside in favor of letting "yes" and "no" suffice. He condemned revenge and set forth the ideal of the other cheek and the second mile. Much argument has raged as to how far we may practice this injunction in the present age but the spirit of the second mile should be in every believer instead of that all too-common "chip-on-the-shoulder" attitude. Impartial love to friend and enemy alike is the Spirit of Christ but, alas, we still love most those from whom we hope to receive.

Our Lord concluded this portion of His discourse by saying, "Be ye therefore perfect, even as your Father which is in heaven is perfect." Here the idea is that of completeness, not sinless perfection. But even at that, the sermon on the mount sets before us an impossible ideal except for Calvary. Idealists and dreamers through the ages have tried to create communities where people lived by the sermon on the mount but the ventures have been pitiful failures. Tolstoi and his colony were examples of this misguided impulse which has led many astray. Many preachers today follow only the Christ of the mount be we can only reach the Mount by way of Calvary. Christ met the demands of the law and it is only Christ living within the believer Who can live out the principles He Himself laid down. As I receive Him by faith and abide in Him the Holy Spirit produces in me the fruits which the Law demanded but could not create. Nothing is more discouraging than the sermon on the mount unless we see it through the light of the cross. Only Christ can meet His own ideals but this He will do in everyone who receives Him. Even then, we believe that the literal application of this sermon awaits the kingdom age to come but the spiritual application is for us now and is met by Christ through the Holy Spirit indwelling the believer.

"Good-For-Nothing Christians"
April 3, 1938

"Ye are the salt of the earth: but if the salt have lost his savour, wherewith shall it be salted? It is thenceforth good for nothing, but to be cast out, and to be trodden under foot of men" Mt. 5:13.

Our Lord used simplest figures of speech. Believers are here set forth as the salt of the earth. The Christian has many saline characteristics. Salt is cleansing and every believer, himself cleansed by the Word and the blood, should cast a purifying influence wherever he goes. Every believer should have an antiseptic influence, the very air should clear up with his presence and conversation. The true social gospel is nothing more or less than the salting of the community with the life and testimony of born-again believers. Sin is disease, sickness, and the only remedy is the Gospel. We are living gospels, epistles known and read of all men and our work is to cleanse and purify by the outliving of Christ within.

Salt is relishing, it gives seasoning flavor. Consider how flat is food that has not been salted. And the believer should have salt in himself (Mk. 9:50) and not be the flat, insipid sort we find composing the greater part of our church memberships. One reason why men pay so little attention to the Gospel today is the tasteless living of Christians. We make our church services as dreary as possible. Many Christians get a negative slant and go about so dead and dull that they repel any who might be considering the claims of Christ. There should be a zest, a relish, a good flavour to our faith that puts color into life and gives it tone and makes it tasty. The average church or Christian today reminds us of bread without salt.

Salt preserves. It keeps from spoiling and putrefaction. Christians are a preservative to society. The world would have been rotten long ago but for the presence of the Holy Spirit in Christians, the salt of the earth. And when Christ takes up His saints, speedy corruption will immediately set in. It is the church that saves the world from decay, little as the world appreciates it.

We read of the savour of the knowledge of Christ (2 Cor. 2:14). It is this that gives the salt its flavour. But the believer can become tasteless and the salt thus loses its savour. The most useless thing in the world is salt without savour. It is good for nothing. Unsavoury meat can be remedied but what can you do with unsavoury salt? We read that the salt without savour is to be cast out and trodden under foot of men. Such is the fate of the castaway who brings upon himself the contempt of even the sinning world because he professes what he does not possess.

Here is a grievous reality in our world today. Think of the thousands of lifeless, tasteless Christians who carry no flavour whatsoever, are insipid and flat. And think of the churches that merely carry on an order of service but are devoid of any seasoning grace. Such are headed for judgment for they are good for nothing else.

Let your life be salted with the knowledge of Christ. Let your speech be with grace seasoned with salt. Don't be a good-for-nothing Christian.

"Faith and Care"
June 24, 1934

Four times in Matthew does our Lord use the expression, "O ye of little faith," and each time the application is to a different problem. The first occurrence of the phrase is in Mt. 6:30: "Wherefore, if God so clothe the grass of the field, which today is, and tomorrow is cast into the oven, shall He not much more clothe you, O ye of little faith?"

This is part of the well-known passage from the Sermon on the Mount dealing with our daily anxieties. Nowhere is faith more needed nowadays. Many Christians seem to think of worry as a "white sin," as though God had made an exception in that case and we were allowed to fret and grieve with no provision made for our relief. People think they simply must worry but God's Word is explicit that we are to be careful for nothing (Phil. 4:6), casting all our care upon God (1 Pt. 5:7), letting not our hearts be troubled (Jn. 14:1). Why say "Let not your heart be troubled" if we cannot help it?

So our Lord tells us: "Take no thought for your life, what ye shall put on. Is not the life more than meat, and the body than raiment?" Of course, we know that "thought" here means anxious care and not that forethought and planning which are necessary for any business. It is not work but worry that kills–the feverish tension and uneasiness that soon wear down mind and body. The man who lives in the will of God need never worry about food, clothes, and the vexations of daily experience. It does no good, it is positively forbidden in the Word, and God has promised to supply all the believer's needs (Phil. 4:19).

The Lord Jesus speaks in this passage of the birds and the lilies as illustrations of God's care. Here cynics have objected that the sparrow falls just the same. But the idea is that, no matter what happens, we are in God's care. The mistake is in limiting His care to temporal welfare but God does not guarantee to save us from trouble and danger. His care goes beyond that: come what will, our lives are hid with Christ and, no matter what happens to our health or our money, we ourselves, our spirits, are safe in Him.

The heart of the whole matter is found in verse 33: "But seek ye first the kingdom of God and His righteousness; and all these things shall be added unto you." We make "all these things" our chief concern but Christ makes them merely incidental. These things should be marginal and God central in our lives but we put them on the main track and God is switched to the side-track to be called upon only in trouble.

"Sufficient unto the day is the evil thereof." Each day has enough troubles of its own. But we insist upon borrow from tomorrow and crossing the bridge before we reach it. No Christian should worry. His sole business is to know the will of God and do it. Whatever his occupation may be, it is only to pay expenses while he is about his real business. But we reverse the whole matter and make our trade the main business with God's will an outside affair that is considered now and then, if at all. Consequently, when trouble and vexation come we fret and worry.

Truly our little faith shows up daily in this matter of care. The believer who has gained through faith the conquest of care has found life here even in this trouble-

"Faith and Care"

---

some world a blessed experience. But, though possible to all, this victory is exceedingly rare because we simply excuse our worrying and feel that the carefree life is not for us. We miss the peace of God which garrisons the hearts and minds of those who are careful for nothing but thankful for everything.

"When Thou Prayest"
July 14, 1935

In the sermon on the mount our Lord reproved all worship done with an eye to the public. Those who so worship "have their reward," they did it to be noticed and notice is what they get. He said little for public prayer but commended the secret place with the closed door. That our Father knows what we need before we ask is not an excuse for not asking, it is here given as an incentive to asking.

The Lord's Prayer is His only in that He gave it to us. He did not need to pray it for it asks for forgiveness which He needed not. But it is a fitting prayer for us and how balanced! There is the worshipful beginning with its adoration; the prayer for His coming kingdom, the general desire that His Will be done on earth; then, the particular requests for daily bread, forgiveness, help in temptation, and the worshipful close with its eternal outlook "for ever."

Jesus cautions us that an unforgiving spirit on our part hinders God forgiving us. Then He holds up the ideal of true riches in heavenly investment where misfortune and depressions cannot reach. We are to have a single purpose, our eye must be single, "this one thing we must do." We cannot serve God and the things of earth.

We are not to live in anxious care about tomorrow, what we shall eat, drink and wear. The birds and the lilies are examples of our Father's provision. The true believer knows God has promised to supply all his needs and he reckons on God's faithfulness. Trusting in the Lord and doing good he dwells in the land and is fed. The things of God are put first and all else is added. Each day has enough troubles of its own.

These admonitions from the sixth chapter of Matthew are familiar. They have been read and memorized and treasured and perhaps no portion of the Bible has been practiced less. Care is the "white sin" of most believers who imagine that worry cannot be prevented. But we are expressly told to cast our care upon Him for He cares for us. The caring is His business but most of us insist on helping Him attend to it.

In the seventh chapter we are bidden not to judge others or to look for faults in others overlooking greater faults in ourselves. Holy and precious truths aren't to be wasted on those incapable of receiving them. We are assured that God answers prayer (verse 7-11.) The golden rule has been misused for only Christians truly can keep it. The way to heaven is narrow and few travel it (13,14). False prophets are to be known by the fruits of their ministry (15-20). It is not lip-worship but obedience that counts (21-23).

Our Lord closed His message with a parable of the house built on sand and the house on the rock. Christ is the sure foundation (1 Cor. 3:11) and lives built on Him shall endure. Where the life is unworthy, the soul is saved if it be on the Rock, but how much better when soul and life are to His glory. "The day shall declare it," the last day will show up all shams and realities (Mal. 3:17, 18.)

"How Are You Building?"
September 5, 1937

Our Lord pointed out in Mt. 7:24-27 the contrast between building on the sand and on the rock. The same storm came to both because in the world the believer is promised tribulation (John 16:33), but he who heard His Lord's words and practiced them stood the test.

In 1 Cor. 3:10-15 we have set before us the solemn responsibility of the believer to be careful about his building. Christ is the only sure foundation, for He is the chief cornerstone (Eph. 2:20), the tried Stone, the sure foundation, (Is. 28:16). But the building must not only be on the Lord but must be built by Him for except the Lord build the house they labor in vain that build it (Ps. 127:1).

God works, however, through consecrated apprentices and here Paul tells us that a man may build upon the true foundation with gold, silver, and precious stones or with wood, hay or stubble. The fire of judgment will test the life and although the believer himself shall be saved, if he have built of wood, hay and stubble his life work shall be destroyed.

Here then is indeed a most serious matter and surely every Christian should take heed how he builds thereon. Consider in our sermon preparation how many times we preachers fill our discourses with wood, hay and stubble when with more prayer and study we might have built a message of gold! Every sermon ought to be our very best under God's direction. And how often have you, Sunday school teacher, hurriedly woven in some stubble of your own interpretation, a block of wood where there might have been silver?

In conversation with the ungodly how often have we talked weather and politics and laughed over trivialities and missed a chance to redeem the time with a word fitly spoken which is like apples of gold in pictures of silver (Prov. 23:11). One day judgment fire will burn through our conversations and so much will go up in smoke!

Think of how we waste spare time, filling it with unenduring materials when we could make it a permanent blessing. We build unworthily, cheaply because we will not pay the price for the best materials. God offers us gold already tried in fire (Rev. 3:18) but there are no bargain rates and reduced prices. It takes hours of prayer and Bible study and obedience and self-denial. If our lifework is to be fire-proof it will not be so built by sentence prayers and one-minute Bible readings before breakfast. It costs, so we slip in a block of wood here and fill in with hay there and get by with stubble yonder.

One day we shall thank God we built with enduring material. That time you waited in intercessory prayer when the devil said, "Go to bed"; and that time you called on a certain person to lead him to Christ though you were ever so nervous; that time you were reconciled to an offended brother; that time you gave ten dollars when Satan suggested fifty cents; that time you gave up that job because it was doubtful in a spiritual way–at such times we build for eternity and the day shall declare it. It is so easy to let up here and there and work in a little wood or stubble but blessed is the man who will not substitute even the good for the best.

How are you building? With gold, silver, precious stones, or with wood, hay and stubble?

"Faith and Fear"
July 1, 1934

In the eighth chapter of Matthew, Jesus says to the alarmed disciples who have wakened Him in the storm at sea: "Why are ye fearful, O ye of little faith?" They had cried out in alarm, "Lord, save us; we perish" according to Matthew; according to Mark: "Master, carest thou not that we perish?"

How true to human nature is that fearfulness of His disciples! After all the mighty works which they had seen Him do, here they could see only the immediate danger. Some have used the sleeping presence of Christ in the boat to indicate that Christ is in every believer and needs only to be called into action by stirring up the gift of God within us. But such an interpretation beclouds the matter. It was fear rather than faith that called upon Him here: a stronger faith would have let Him sleep. There is more faith in a quiet dependence upon the indwelling Christ than in an excitable anxiousness that would awaken Him in every storm as though any real harm could come to us when He is within.

Many believers need to learn that faith delivers from fear. Theoretically, we believe in the Christ within but when the crisis comes, we grow panicky and cry, "Master, we perish!" But faith and fear are contradictory. In proportion as we have one we do not have the other. "There is no fear in love; but perfect love casteth out fear; because fear hath torment. He that feareth is not made perfect in love" (1 John 4:18). Since love is the outward working of faith it follows that faith, working by love, drives out fear.

How the Master would cry to us timid and alarmed disciples as He did to these: "Why are ye fearful, O ye of little faith?" "How is it that ye have no faith?" "Where is your faith?" No Christian need fear anything "for God hath not given us the spirit of fear; but of power, and of love and of a sound mind" (2 Tim. 1:7). We fear misfortune; we fear criticism; we fear others; we fear to undertake things, to speak for Christ; we fear for financial security; we fear sickness; we cross bridges before we reach them; we fear the future. But for every fear "faith is the victory."

We are not thinking of fear merely as a feeling but as an attitude that paralyzes the will and restrains and cramps the life until one becomes a cowering slave. Neither is faith merely a feeling but the attitude which steps forth in dependence upon God even though feelings and circumstances may point the other way. The conquest of fear is not wrought in a day. The Christian who sets out to live by faith will find many nervous qualms and inhibitions trying to choke his courage but as he exercises faith the faith grows stronger and the fear weaker until it no longer becomes a serious problem. Here as everywhere else the practice of His presence plays its part.

Some believers make the mistake of waiting until they feel all fear disappear before they venture forth by faith. But they never reach the high hills that way. Faith sets out in the very teeth of adverse circumstances and contrary feelings and makes fear disappear by continually assuming, asserting and practicing the attitude of faith until it becomes real and fear has been broken. Of course, it is all done through the indwelling Spirit but still there must be practice and persistence. God will empower and sustain but the decision

"Faith and Fear"

of the will is our part and all the prayers and devotional readings on earth will not make up for our definite stepping out upon the promises.

"The Healer"
May 12, 1935

Our Lord's ministry was threefold, teaching, preaching, and healing. Matthew lists different classes of sick, those taken with diverse disease and torments, the devil possessed, lunatics, those who had palsy, and adds "and He healed them." No case was too difficult.

We read that they were astonished at His doctrine "for His word was with power." We have that same message which is to be given in demonstration of the Spirit and of power but, alas, few are astonished today. It is not that they have become accustomed to it. The trouble is, it is not preached with power, "with the Holy Ghost sent down from heaven" (1 Peter 1:12.) Once again the bench-warmers in the pews would sit up and take notice and hungry souls would be fed and sinners convicted if we recovered that note of authority. But we speak as the scribes, there is the dreary monotone of the academic, the deaf reputation of dry platitudes; there is not Jeremiah's bone-fire of silence.

Even demons recognized our Lord's authority. These demoniacs were not merely crazy people. Demon possession is real for here it is the demon who cries out with a loud voice (Mark 1:26) and there is a distinction made between the possessor and the possessed. The word of God is still able to defeat the devil but today we stand at the foot of the mountain like the disciples in failure before a devil-possessed world. Our note of authority is gone and we are not defeating the devil. Our Lord said the power came by prayer and fasting. Of course we are told that this verse is an interpolation but certainly the truth of it is undeniable. Our note of authority over evil is lacking because prayer is lacking.

Our Lord proves His power over disease by the healing of Peter's wife's mother. Then follows (Mt. 8:15, 17; Mk. 1:32-34; Lk. 4:40, 41) a sunset scene of healing which stands out in the three Synoptics. Worthy of any painters best efforts this lovely picture must have been, the sick and weary multitudes pressing upon Him at the close of day and coming away well and strong again. We have grown accustomed to reading such records but think what a sensation if that should be today!

Mark and Luke add another incident that shows the other side of this ministry of power. In the morning He rose a great while before day and departed into a solitary place and there prayed. He knew that if He was to give forth power He must receive power from the Father. If He needed so to pray, how can we expect to minister in power without the early retreat to the solitary place? There is the secret of powerlessness, "If he be alone there is tidings in his mouth." There must be solitude if there is to be a testimony of power, Elijah, must hide himself before he can show himself to Ahab.

Peter finds our Lord in prayer and says "All men seek for thee." How we would have returned to the popularity and the plaudits, indeed we would likely never have left them! But our Lord knew what was in man and that He must move on where He was sent. How easy for us to forget orders in the flush of success. Like Abraham's servant let us suffer no man to hinder us when God has prospered our way.

"As Thou Hast Believed"
March 26, 1939

In Mt. 8:5-13 we have the account of the healing of the centurion's servant. Centurions figure prominently in the New Testament. There was the one at the cross who said, "Truly this was the Son of God." There was Cornelius, the Gentile convert.

First, this centurion showed concern. He came beseeching Jesus for his servant who was probably a favorite and a valuable man. If we are to receive anything from the Lord for ourselves or others, we must be concerned. "No man cared for my soul" might well be a test for a sermon entitled, "Who Cares?" There are salesmen selling toothpaste and hair tonic over the radio with more zeal than many of us are preaching the Gospel. And now many parents and friends today are coming to Jesus with the needs of their loved ones, concerned half as much as this centurion over his servant?

Next, he showed contrition. He told the Lord, "I am not worthy that thou shouldest come under my roof." Today people argue, "I didn't ask to be born; God ought to save me." We read such signs as "Your soul will be saved if you make it worth saving." But if we are to be blessed of Jesus, we must come as beggars, deserving nothing. Jacob, faced with a crisis, prayed, "I am not worthy of the least of all the mercies and of all the truth with Thou hast shewed unto Thy servant." John the Baptist was a fearless preacher but he could say of Jesus, "Whose shoes I am not worthy to bear." The prodigal son had to be humbled to say, "I am not worthy to be called Thy son."

Then the centurion showed confidence. He asked Jesus merely to speak the word and his servant would be healed. Jesus said, "As thou hast believed, so be it done unto thee." Faith is the only hand that can receive anything from God. Without faith we cannot please God. Jesus complimented this man's faith. Jesus always told those whom He blessed that their faith had done it. We keep thinking that there is some other key to blessing but it is simply according to our faith.

Then, the centurion obeyed Jesus and went his way. He showed conformity to our Lord's command. He took the word for the deed and went home to find it so. Hannah took God's word and went her way with her countenance no more sad. When Jesus cursed the fig tree, He did not stay there to see whether it died or not. He went His way and when He came back, it was dead and He used that to tell His disciples that when they prayed they were to believe they had what they prayed for and they should have it (Mk. 11:24). We say that God is able to help us and we hope He will but Jesus says God has done the thing we ask for in faith and we are to go on believing it. As the lepers went they were cleansed and so are we.

Finally, there was confirmation. When the centurion reached home he found the servant healed. Of course he did! It is always as the Lord says. When the Zarephath widow obeyed Elijah, I read "And the barrel of meal wasted not, neither did the cruse of oil fail, according to the word of the Lord which he spake by Elijah." When the disciples went to prepare the place of the Lord's Supper, they found as He had said. It is always so. The faith which believes shall see!

March 19, 1939

Three times this phrase is used in the New Testament with meanings very precious to us. In Mt. 8:23-27, our Lord asleep in a boat and awakened by His disciples when a storm arose, rebuked the waves and then His disciples for their lack of faith. They marveled, saying, "What manner of man is this, that even the winds and the sea obey Him!"

Indeed, a new kind of man came to earth in Jesus Christ. None other had ever lived and spoken and died and risen like Him. A new race began with Jesus Christ. He was Son of Man and Son of God, the Word made flesh, Emmanuel. The old race was a failure and God chose Israel as the channel for a new Adam. The first Adam was innocent; the new Adam was perfect, sinless. The world has marveled through the ages concerning Christ, "What manner of man is this?" But the world has not seen that He is the Adam of a new race, not merely a teacher, a prophet, but a new man, a God-man. In this light, it is no wonder that He was virgin-born. How could it have been otherwise? The very facts demanded it.

But had He stood alone and had there been no way that we could enter into this truth, it would help us none at all to contemplate Him. So the word goes on to say: "Behold, what manner of love the Father hath bestowed upon us that we should be called the sons of God" (1 John 3:1). Thank God, I may be a member of this new race! That is the meaning of the new birth. Christ is not an isolated phenomenon in the course of history. He was the "firstborn among many brethren" (Rom. 8:29). I may be a brother with Him in the new race, born from above through faith in Him. I cannot take out naturalization papers and get into it. Nicodemus was a religious man but he must be born again. The reason why we have so much trouble with some church members is because they never have become members of God's family. They belong to their father, the devil and the lusts of their father they will do, so they are a problem when they get into a church. You know what to do with your own family but when a neighbor's boy or girl comes over, you sometimes are at a loss as to him or her.

When I trust Christ as Savior, I enter a new race with God my Father and Jesus my elder brother and I am saved that I might be conformed to the image of God's Son. So it is logical to consider another occurrence of the phrase with which we started: "Seeing then that all these things shall be dissolved, what manner of persons ought we to be in all holy conversation and godliness" (2 Pet. 3:11). That reminds us of the last part of 1 John 3:1: "Therefore the world knoweth us not because it knew Him not." Does the world know you? Too many professing Christians are better known to the world than to the church. Arguing about card-playing, dancing, etc., often proceeds on a mistaken basis. There is just one thing that forever settles such things: they simply don't belong to the family of God. Born-again Christians do not practice sin because "his seed remaineth" in us and we cannot sin because we are born of God (1 John 3:9). I believe in this kind of family pride.

But the reason here given is that we are in the last days and should behave accordingly. We do not belong to the world. May we live in keeping with our new family name!

"The Gadarene"
September 22, 1935

After mastering a wild sea the Lord Jesus masters a wild man. Three Gospels give us the story of the Gadarene demoniac (Mt. 8:28-34; Mk. 5:1-20; Lk. 8:26-39) and it is unusual that Mark's account, usually the briefest, is here the longest.

There are those who would make this man to be only an insane case but our Lord clearly recognized demon-possession by His saying, "Come out of the man, thou unclean spirit." That He was merely accepting the common view of His time is an argument too foolish to reserve room for refutation.

Much has been said about the destruction of the swine who refused to endure what men put up with. Huxley made much of this destruction of property as an argument against the Lord. Our Lord never went at anything tamely. He made bold strokes and brushed everything else aside to get at a needy life. What are a few hogs to a human soul? The destruction of the swine was a bold evidence of the miracle and a daring declaration that lives are ever more important than property. If the owner of the hogs had accepted the Lord Jesus he would have had a treasure inestimable. Instead he saw only temporal loss and gain and because Jesus was hurting his business he besought Him to leave.

Men have followed that procedure through the ages. When Christ interferes with our personal gain we usually beseech Him to leave.

There is a beautiful truth in the healed man's desire to go with the Lord and His disciples in the ship to other parts. Doubtless he wanted to get away from the scenes of his past and it looked very inviting, this prospect of sojourning with the Lord in new fields ever hearing His words and witnessing His miracles. But it was not so to be: he must stay in the old, unromantic spot and tell what the Lord has done for his soul (and what a witness he must have been!)

Many of us have known this experience. We have longed to follow the Lord across the sea or in some more interesting field but He has commissioned us to stay at home, live down an evil past perhaps and be an obscure and unknown witness. It is not give into everyone to go far afield; there must be the disciple who stayed at home. Time and time again we meet with those who went to foreign fields or undertook vast enterprises under mistaken leadings. It is so easy to confuse our wants with God's leadings. The work of the gospel is too often made the springboard from which to dive off into water too deep for us.

This man obeyed the Lord's command and as he proclaimed his story men marveled according to Marks' account. Together with a marvelous experience of deliverance he had an obedient spirit and that makes a great combination.

Are you willing that Christ should do His wonders in your life at any cost to property and circumstances? Then are you willing to let Him station you where He will to be His witness?

"According to Your Faith"
October 6, 1935

After the raising of Jairus' daughter our Lord on His departure was followed by two blind men crying for mercy (Mt. 9:27-34.) He asked them, "Believe ye that I am able to do this?" And they answered, "Yes, Lord." Then He touched their eyes, saying, "According to your faith be it unto you" and their eyes were opened.

A simple story, so simple that we pass over it and overlook its tremendous revelation. Here is the key to a life of blessing. "According to your faith." But, mind you, faith in the Lord Jesus, for He had just asked, ""Believe ye that I am able to do this?" The value of faith depends upon the object of faith and when Christ is the object faith never fails. All things are possible to him that believeth if he believes in Him with Whom all things are possible.

Back of all the misery of the world today lies unbelief in Christ. We will not come unto Him that we might have life. Sinners miss life here and hereafter because they believe not and Christians live meagre and defeated lives because they believe so little. In the midst of it all stands Jesus, the answer to every problem, but we do not believe like the blind men that he is able to do wonders in our lives or, if we believe it theoretically, we do not believe it practically so our eyes are not opened. Some seek special experiences, signs and wonders, but will not live daily by faith looking unto Jesus.

Here is the measure of blessing. According to your faith. If there is much faith there is much blessing. If there is little faith there is little blessing. There is no other way. Simple faith in Jesus Christ is the key to every problem, the answer to every issue from the smallest to the greatest. He Himself said so: how long will it take us to learn it?

After this miracle the Lord healed a dumb demoniac and the Pharisees attributed His miracle to the devil. Alas, there are religious people today who deny a God of miracles and ascribe works of healing to the devil! It is to the everlasting shame of the church that we have lost sight of Christ the Healer and stand almost in the place of the Pharisees ridiculing those who have the gift of healing plainly taught in the New Testament and almost ascribing the work of God to Beelzebub.

Our Lord went next to Nazareth and there what struck Him was unfaith. His townspeople were offended in Him and He could do no mighty works there because of their unbelief. He marveled at the centurious faith (Mt. 8:10) but here He marveled at their unbelief (Mk. 6:6.) So we read that He went around about the village teaching. He was restricted to a teaching ministry here and so He is today in most places for we believe not. What wonders might not come to pass if we only believed!

"New Wine in Old Bottles"
May 26, 1935

The synoptic Gospels record in detail the call of Matthew the publican and the dinner that followed in his home. The story of his call is brief but sufficient. Our Lord passed by and said, "Follow me" and he arose and followed Him. If Jesus had been aiming at popularity He would never have summoned this despised tax collector to be one of the twelve. But our Lord saw in him the writer of a gospel and present station meant nothing. It is significant that Christ called a busy man.

The call was followed by dinner at Matthew's house where the scribes and Pharisees were offended at His eating with publicans and sinners. He answers with irony: the publicans are sick and know it and have availed themselves of the Great Physician; the Pharisees think they have no need of Christ. He declares that He came to call sinners to repentance and not the righteous, not meaning that the Pharisees were righteous but that, since they thought themselves so, He did not expect them to welcome Him. It parallels His statement in John 9:39: "For judgement I am come into this world, that they which see not might see; and that they which see might be made blind." "The rich He sent empty away."

Our Lord justifies His action by quoting Hosea 6:6: "I will have mercy and not sacrifice." How we need to go and learn experimentally what much of the Word means! How terrible to be a stickler for form and observance and know not that love and mercy without which religion is but a hollow farce!

Then followed the question about feasting and fasting, why John's disciples fasted and Jesus' disciples feasted. Our Lord compares Himself and His disciples to a bridal party. When the Bridegroom has gone it will be time enough to fast. Notice it is the disciples of John who raise this question instigated by the Pharisees; how readily the devil uses any apparent rift among disciples to further his own ends! Our Lord's skillful answer cast no reproach on John's disciples yet vindicated His own.

Then He uses the figure of new cloth on an old garment and new wine in old bottles, skin bottles of course being in mind. In other words the practices of John's disciples were suited to his teaching and so were those of Christ's disciples; and nay attempt to mix them or graft the practices of one upon the other would be harmful. To patch up the Judaism of John with the new observances of Christ would make a mongrel mixture. The new practices, the greater liberties of Christ's disciple befit the new dispensation. Luke adds a peculiar statement (5:39): "No man also having drunk old wine straightway desireth new; for he saith, The old is better." Do not expect men long accustomed to Judaism to change overnight. We must not expect too sudden a change to new doctrine. Here is a warning to all who have no patience with tradition and want immediate and "straightway" acceptance to new truths. Be patient: in due time the new wine will become old. Nothing is more needful than that we shall be considerate of those who have long cherished another viewpoint. We can be too hasty with them and we must not demand instantaneous overnight sympathy with new practices. Practice must bring familiarity and in due time the new wine will taste better.

"Dawn From the Mountain"
December 15, 1935

From the mountain-top of transfiguration the Lord leads the disciples down the road to practical service. He finds the other disciples powerless to cast out a demon from a possessed youth. The desperate father pleads, "If thou canst do any thing, have compassion on us and help us." Jesus answers, "If thou canst believe, all things are possible to him that believeth." It reminds us of His word to the blind men, "According to your faith be it unto you." (Mt. 9:29.)

How poorly we have learned this lesson! Our faith is the measure of our blessing. Today faith is being extolled for its own sake as though it mattered not what we believe, just so we believe something with all our might. So we are told that prayer is valuable for its own reflex action upon the one who prays. But the value of faith depends upon the object of faith. All things are possible to him that believeth if he believes in Him with Whom all things are possible.

But when the Lord is the object of faith then the measure of blessing and achievement is in proportion to that faith. Truly we need to cry out today as did the father of this boy, "Lord, I believe: help thou mine unbelief!"

Our Lord reproves the faithless disciples and declares that such goes not out but by prayer and fasting. If we accept the consensus of scholars that this verse is not in the original, the fact remains that we do not have such power and such faith and we still believe that it comes the way of prayer and most of us would do well to change from feasting to fasting.

There are plenty of demons to be cast out today, demons entrenched in the soul and societies and men but we lack the power. We speak not with authority. Christians and churches stand embarrassed and defeated before the modern demoniacs. When Sir Thomas Aquinas visited the Vatican, the Pope said as they viewed the splendors: "No longer does the church have to say, 'Silver and gold have I none.'" "True," answered Aquinas, "but neither can she say, 'Rise and walk'!"

To this passage (Mt. 17:14-23; Mk. 9:14-32; Lk. 9:37-45) Matthew adds the incident of the coin in the fishes mouth. The tax was due and our Lord could have claimed exemption as Son of God but He was willing to forego His rights and pay it by a miracle. We Christians may learn a needed lesson there. There are many obligations from which we may feel exempt but rather than offend others it is best to meet them. There are many little duties which often are irksome and which strictly speaking, do not bind us but we are still in the world and must forego personal privilege time and again so long as no principle is involved. If the King of glory was willing to be bothered with so small a matter as temple-tax we should not grow too important to overlook such small items. Notice our Lord said to Peter, "Give unto them for me and thee." The Lord shares with His servant! If He is with us He shares life's ordinary cares, even our taxes!

"According to Your Faith"
June 17, 1934

Worlds of possibilities are wrapped up in our Lord's statement to the blind men in Mt. 9:29: "According to your faith be it unto you."

Men go from book to book, from lecture to lecture, seeking a more abundant life. Weak Christians devour devotional literature always expecting that the next page will unlock the mystic secret. But here is the key: faith grows as we exercise such faith as we have. Here is the measure of the life abundant, just in proportion to our faith. God's resources are ever available to faith. If we make our check small we have only ourselves to blame.

Observe that it is not "according to your fate." The Chinese have a proverb: "We make our fortune and call it Fate." Some of us excuse our laziness under the guise of predestination and say "what is to be will be." Nor is it "according to your fortune." Lands and goods are not the measure of life abundant for "a man's life consisteth not in the abundance of the things which he possesses" (Lk. 12:15). It is not "according to your fame" for the celebrities are often most miserable. As Johnson said, Fame usually comes when we are old and can't enjoy it, solitary and can't share it, independent and don't need it. Christ did not say, "According to your friends." Popularity and "pull" cannot bring us life abundant. Too many friends are like shadows, they follow us only on sunny days. Nor did our Lord say, "According to your feelings." There is the commonest mistake in looking for a better life. We confuse it with certain emotional ecstasies and are discouraged when feelings rise and fall and moods change like April weather.

It is "according to your faith." But here we need to examine just what sort of faith this is for faith itself has been made a fetish with those who think faith alone is sufficient, no matter what we believe. The value of faith depends upon its object. If the object of confidence turns out unworthy the one who believed is in worse condition than before, no matter how worthy his faith may have been. Popular teaching which puts the emphasis upon faith itself makes it purely subjective while the real virtue lies in the object.

The only faith which brings eternal life and a more abounding daily experience is faith in the Lord Jesus Christ for He only is worthy of absolute trust and able to meet every need of the believer. "Believe on the Lord Jesus Christ" was the early message of the apostles and simple faith in Christ as Son of God and Saviour is the condition of salvation. Then more abounding life and growth are "according to our faith." If we believe only to a small degree, our experience will be commensurate to that faith. Every believer has found that, as far as he trusted, he found the promises true.

So, do not look for something magical about this matter of faith. Your experience will be in proportion as you take God at His Word, in spite of all appearances. But the value of faith lies in Him Whom you trust, not on the quantity nor quality of your faith. "All things are possible to him that believeth" if he believes in Him with Whom all things are possible.

Here and here only is the way to life victorious and abundant for "this is the victory that overcometh the world, even our faith" (1 John 5:4).

"The Twelve Sent Forth"
October 13, 1935

The sending forth of the disciples upon their first preaching tour (Mt. 10; Mk. 6:7-13; Lk. 9:1-6) has been the favorite pretext of misguided fanatics through the centuries. Time and again, some erratic soul has taken these commands literally and endeavored to practice them even to the point of the sandals and staff. They overlook the very first statement of our Lord in Matthew's account, that this mission was purely local and temporary, to the lost sheep of the house of Israel. Later on (Lk. 22:35, 36) when they must face a hostile Gentile world, they are given entirely different instructions and bidden to provide themselves with swords.

But it is also true that in Matthew's account, further on in our Lord's discourse, (v. 16-23) He seems to go beyond the immediate application a prophecy the trials and persecutions which they later underwent after His ascension. There we have an application that stretches through all the Gospel age.

Next He says: "Ye shall not have gone over the cities of Israel till the Son of man be come." While there is a sense in which Christ "came" in the destruction of Jerusalem or even earlier in the empowering of the Spirit of Pentecost, we are looking here at the ministry of the faithful remnant of Israel in the last days before our Lord's second advent. The disciples pre-figured the faithful witnesses in the time of Israel's great trouble before our Lord comes in judgment.

The rest of Jesus' message to the twelve contains general principles applicable to any age. What He had declared to them privately must be proclaimed aloud without fear of men who could destroy only the body. There our Lord declares that He came not to bring peace but a sword and that He is the great divider, separating even families in their allegiance to or rejection of Him. In these days when light and easy things are being said of our Lord and He is pictured as the Great Pacifist with a gospel of brotherhood, sweetness and light, we need to remember that really Jesus Christ has been and is the most devising force in all history. He that is not with Him is against Him and he that gathers not with Him scatters abroad and with the sharp, two-edged sword of the Word, Jesus Christ splits the whole human race asunder to the right and to the left, He unifies those who are in Him but He is the great Divider of humanity and this age will see division to the end over the supreme issue. Where do we stand with regard to Christ? His Gospel is the savor of life unto life or of death unto death and by Him the thoughts of all men are revealed.

Although many of the literal commands of this commission of the twelve are not for us, it would be a great day if His witnesses now so comfortably settled in established positions could go forth with the abandon of these early missionaries. Alas, with too many of us, the adventure of the Cross has become a fixed professionalism. We need the old abandon of those who having freely received freely gave.

"Warnings and Invitations"
July 28, 1935

In Mt. 11:20-30 our Lord reaches one of the cross-roads in His ministry. Hitherto He has preached to the lost sheep of the house of Israel the gospel of the kingdom, offering Himself as the long-expected Messiah. But Israel has refused Him so now He pronounces judgment upon them and turns to the world at large with a general invitation to all who are weary, the labouring and the laden, to come to Him for rest.

It is a remarkable fulfillment of prophecy that the cities here condemned lie today in ruins. Chorazin, Bethsaida, and Capernaum are mute witnesses to the truth of this judgment. That it would be "more tolerable" for Sodom and Tyre and Sidon indicates that there will be degrees of punishment.

Then our Lord thanked God that the deeper truths were hidden from the wise and prudent and revealed unto babes. It has ever been so, the wise in their own conceits pass the Gospel by while the simple receive it. Only those who abandon their pride and become childlike can enter the kingdom. If it were otherwise men would take credit for being saved and flesh would glory in His presence.

Then follows one of those sublime statements that show the resources of our Lord: "All things are delivered unto me of the Father; and no man knoweth the Son but the Father;

neither knoweth any man the Father, save the Son and he to whomsoever He will reveal Him." Here all things belong to Jesus and Paul says all things are ours (1 Cor. 3:21-23) for we are joint-heirs with Christ. In this passage all things are Christ's and He says "Come." In John, 3:35-36 all things His and He says "Believe." In Mt. 28:18-20 all things are His and He says "Go."

Having first stated His resources Jesus then invites the labouring and laden to come to Him. Since all belong to these classes all are invited. Notice He says He will give us rest but in the next verse He bids us learn of Him and find rest. Rest is both an obtainment and an attainment. Positionally, we receive His rest when we come to Him. But, conditionally, in experience this rest is ours daily as we abide in Him and learn of Him. It is not earned but it is learned. Heb. 4:9-11 bears the same thought concerning His rest. He that is entered into God's rest has ceased from his own works, yet the next verse bids us labor to enter into that rest. His yoke is not an extra burden to add to our others but it is meant to make all our burdens lighter. Perhaps the collar of the disciple is meant here rather than the yoke upon a beast of burden.

Those who would reduce the Christian experience to a tedious round of observances and restrictions forget that His yoke is easy and His burden light. Our faith is not weights but wings. Coming to Him, rest is ours as we practice His rest it becomes our condition as well as our position.

"Three Kinds of Burdens"
September 16, 1934

The burden business has been misunderstood and overworked by all too many believers. There are those who invent extra loads and devise all sorts of excess luggage, who think it a mark of exceptional piety to slave through life with uprolled eyes beneath a ton of baggage. Such souls mistake their own petty burdens for the cross of Christ and moan dismally about their load. Job said, "I am a burden to myself" and so are these self-appointed martyrs. What a dour time one has trying to live with such specialists of gloom who never have learned that the spirit-life is not weights but wings!

The Master spoke of the Pharisees, the orthodox religionists of His day, as binding heavy burdens and grievous to be borne, and laying them on men's shoulders while they themselves would not move them with one of their fingers (Mt. 23:4). Many there are whose religious life is only a dull routine of formal observances, the shadow without the substance, "faultily faultless, icily regular, splendidly null," a ritualism without redemption. A load instead of a life!

The Word speaks of three kinds of burdens of which we must dispose. There is, first, the burden we share, "Bear ye one another's burdens, and so fulfill the law of Christ" (Gal. 6:2). Whatever we lift lifts us and as we get under our brother's load with him we find that our own is lightened. The early church had all things in common. We have departed somewhat from that early church ideal but we, at least, ought to have in common those burdens which we can share.

Then, there is the burden we bear. "For every man shall bear his own burden" (Gal. 6:5). There is no conflict here with the other verse just above, as so many have supposed. Here Paul is speaking of our load of personal responsibility which no man can saddle off on someone else. There are obligations which no other man can carry for us.

But the highest summit is reached in Ps. 55:22: "Cast thy burden upon the Lord, and He shall sustain thee." That reminds us of 1 Peter 5:7, "Casting all your care upon Him; for He careth for you." How many trust God with their souls but never with their burdens! The conquest of care is not a matter of fighting them but of surrendering them. Victory here begins with surrender.

Nor is there conflict between bearing our own burden of responsibility and casting our burden upon the Lord. While there are obligations we must assume we must remember that God carries both ourself and our burden. So, the whole load is His; yet, there is a load that is ours.

The lightest hearts are not those who acknowledge no responsibility but those who share and bear burdens, trusting in the Lord. The tracks on the main railroad lines stay shiny for they bear burdens; the sidetracks are rusty for few loads come that way.

Paul says this burden-bearing is "the law of Christ." But that means no heavy and irksome thing. Jesus said "My yoke is easy." Now a yoke is not an extra burden but a device to make the burden light. Our faith is not to be lugged along as an extra obligation like our insurance or taxes; rather, it makes life portable.

Finally, the Master said, "My burden is light." That sums it all. His requirements are not heavy and enslaving.

"Three Kinds of Burdens"

Indeed, He invites all the heavy-laden to Him to find rest. And He follows up that invitation by speaking of His yoke and burden. It might sound contradictory, off-hand, to invite a man to rest and then begin talking about yokes and burdens. But His yoke produces rest and His burden lightens one's load. For His Law brings liberty. "The truth shall set you free." "And you shall find rest unto your soul."

"The Sower"
August 25, 1935

In the thirteenth chapter of Matthew our Lord reaches a turning point in His teaching. He had come to the Jew first, to the lost sheep of the house of Israel and had presented Himself as the Messiah and they had refused Him. He then presents in parable form the mystery of the Gospel in the church age had not been revealed to the prophets having been kept secret from the beginning as our Lord plainly stated (Mt. 13:35.) He spoke in parables that His disciples might catch the deeper meanings while blinded Jews, as Isaiah had prophesied, would hear but not understand.

These parables do not teach world-conversion but rather the saving of a few and a final judgment and separation. The parable of the sower, interpreted by our Lord Himself, shows only one-fourth of the sown seed of the Word taking permanent root. Four types of human soil are presented: the superficial upon whom no lasting impression is made; the emotional, making a fine start but not persevering; the preoccupied, soon choked out by earthly cares; and the truly receptive and productive. Here is encouragement in preaching for, at least, one out of four will receive the seed and bear fruit. Yet here is warning against expecting universal acceptance of the Gospel for the three other types will last until the end.

The Word of God will not return void for it will accomplish His purpose but we must ever remember that it does not profit unless it is mixed with faith (Heb. 4:2). There are those who do not understand it and who do not care nor try to understand it as did the eunuch. They give no earnest heed to the things which they have heard, they go to church and sit politely as did the people before Ezekiel (Ez. 33:30-33) they hear but heed not, and the devil ever watchful, snatches away the word before they get home from church.

Then there are those of the stony ground, who go further than the first group. They receive the Word, a good beginning is made, but they do not hold fast that which is good. They taste the good word of God but while they endure for a while they do not endure until the end. When trouble which works for the faithful a far more exceeding and eternal weight of glory drives these to fall away.

The third kind also springs up, there is a beginning made, but worldly cares distract as they did Martha so that she neglected the main thing. The deceitfulness of riches, the love of money which is the root of all evil, soon chokes the Word and the young enquirer goes away grieved having great possessions–and having nothing! It is hard for a rich man to enter the kingdom because of the exceeding danger of earthly cares and fortunes.

The true believer hears the Word, understands it, being taught of the Spirit. He is also a fruitful believer although there are degrees of fruitfulness. Their hearts are honest and good and they bring forth fruit with patience (Lk. 8:15.)

Therefore we should take heed how we hear; for whosoever hath, to him shall be given; and whosoever hath not, from him shall be taken even that which he seemeth to have (Lk. 8:18).

"Not Law But Love"
December 17, 1939

"An honest and good heart"—Our Lord's parable of the sower in Matthew 13 is fairly familiar as a Sunday school lesson but not so real in actual appreciation of its searching message. Every preacher ought to remember that he has four kinds of soil before him when he preaches lest he be unduly discouraged if all fail to bear fruit.

Our old adversaries, the world, the flesh and the devil are in evidence in this parable, but the order is reversed. The devil comes first stealing away the seed sown by the wayside. He is the thief of sermons as well as the souls and is ever at church. Those who do not understand the Word are simply those who make no effort to understand it. The trouble is not ignorance or inability to understand, for then the fault would not be theirs. They are not in earnest, they merely come to church and hear and go away. The message went in one ear and out the other, and often there is little between the ears to stop it! It is true that the Word is spiritually discerned but these are not willing to be made spiritual, they do not give more earnest heed and the Word does not profit them, not being mixed with faith. What booty they are for the devil and how quickly he snatches away the seed!

Then there are those who hear the Word and receive it with joy. They not only hear, the Word makes an impression.

They swallow it whole, but they merely "enjoy the sermon," and, while they may excitedly make a move, they have no real principle, and their profession fails for lack of perseverance. These lack "patient continuance" and fail to "continue in the perfect law of liberty," though they joyfully look therein. Tribulation and persecution show them up, and they are soon offended. Theirs is weakness of the flesh.

Others hear the Word but the care of this world and the deceitfulness of riches, just as it is not money but the love of money that God warns against. Here it is not the World that hinders the Word.

But, thank God, there is the good soil. There are those who with an honest and good heart receive the Word (Lk. 8:15) and they bear fruit in different degrees. Some are more faithful than others but the heart is honest and they mean business.

Along with this, one thinks of Hosea 10:12: "Break up your fallow ground." Good ground must be broken. There is fallow ground that looks very solid and permanent, but it never can be productive until it has been plowed. Only weeds and thorns grow on fallow ground. There is much preaching today that is wasting the seed on ground that never has been prepared and God tells us not to do that (Jer. 4:3). There is much prayer for showers of blessing that is amiss for God will not waste showers on fallow ground. Christians and churches today do not like to be disturbed, they do not want the plow put it but there can be no harvest without it. There is much talk about revival that overlooks this fact. The broken and contrite heart is God's accepted sacrifice on our part. It takes broken clouds to give rain and broken clods to bear fruit.

Do not look for harvest without first breaking up the ground.

"An Enemy Hath Done This"
September 1, 1935

The parable of the tares throws clear light on a number of issues. Interpreted by our Lord Himself it plainly declares that the world will not be converted in this age: good and evil shall exist together until the end. Thus it destroys that dream of men who imagine a world brotherhood to be created by the preaching of the Gospel which shall set up in this age the reign of universal righteousness.

This parable declares the distinct personality of the devil. Sin is not imperfect goodness, biological growing pains, "An enemy hath done this." Moreover, there is to be a fixed and final separation of good from evil, the wicked gathering for burning, the righteous to shine as the sun in the Father's kingdom as Daniel long before had seen (Dan. 12:3.) The seed here is not the Word, as in the parable of the sower but rather what the Word produces, the children of the kingdom, and the tares are the children of evil. They may get into the churches and look like Christians but they have another nature.

The sowing of tares was done "while men slept." The devil gets his works done today while ministers are asleep, he sows evil the churches while they are taken up with their own ease. He sows in homes while parents sleep, careless of their children's welfare. He sows abroad in the land while rulers who should have an eye to the public welfare look to their own comfort. Then, we read the evil sower "went his way." So goes the devil stealthily about gliding in and out and on his way.

Mind you, this is not a description of the world in general but of Satan's work in the professing church. The field indeed is the world but the sphere of action here is the professing kingdom. We cannot separate the false and true for we cannot read men's hearts. Some who appear righteous are but hypocrites and some who appear wicked are truly saved but not walking in the spirt, God will attend to the final dividing, vengeance is His.

It is possible in church discipline to overstep our boundaries and attempt a separation beyond our right. However, there is little danger of that today for few churches exert as much authority as is their right. But we must be careful lest in ridding ourselves of offenders we root up the good also.

The old emphasis upon a final gathering has disappeared from much of our preaching. But our Lord will gather His wheat (Mt. 3:12) when He takes up His church (1 Thess. 4:13-18.) His reapers, the angels, shall also gather out all that offend and the wicked. Mind you, it is our Lord Himself Who declares the judgment of the wicked to be a furnace of fire (Mt. 13:42) with wailing and gnashing of teeth. He said more about hell than anyone else in the Bible.

"The Kingdom in Parable"
September 8, 1935

After the parables of the sower and the tares, our Lord gave several shorter parables about the Kingdom. Much argument has raged about the interpretation. The mustard-seed and leaven, for instance, are largely held to describe the outward and inward growth of the kingdom from small beginnings to tremendous magnitude reaching over all the world.

Others believe, however, that the mustard-seed represents the rapid but abnormal growth of Christendom, with false believers like the fowls finding refuge in its branches. The leaven is held to represent evil working in and permeating the visible church with false doctrine. Some may hold this view of the leaven to obviate the other alternative of its teaching world conversion. But it would not be necessary to draw world conversion from the phrase, "till the whole was leavened." The Gospel has permeated the world with the influence of its Christ although certainly the world will not be converted. The meal here does not become entirely leaven. The statement, "The Kingdom of heaven is like unto leaven" makes it hard for some to believe that it would have been so worded if leaven means false doctrine.

The parable of the treasure is held to represent Christ for Whom we give up and suffer the loss of all things that we may win Him. Others hold that Israel is the hid treasure and that our Lord buys or redeems it with His own blood. Israel is hidden or lost in the present age, scattered throughout the world. One day the nation is to be reclaimed and restored.

The pearl is also held to typify Christ while men seek goodly pearls. He who seeks this pearl must give up all to possess it. Again, others hold that the church is meant, Christ the merchantman Who gave Himself for the church that He might present it to Himself (Eph. 5:22-23.) It is held that the church, like the pearl, is formed by secretion, not mechanically but vitally through a living one, Christ, Who adds to His church.

The drag-net again sets forth the fact that good and evil will be collected into the professing church to be separated at the end of the age. The truth of a final separation has been obscured in these days but there is no room in these parables for the idea that gradually all men will be won by the Gospel and the world will be Christianized. "The morning cometh and also the night," the good grow better, the bad worse.

Our Lord concluded by saying, "Therefore, every scribe which is instructed unto the kingdom of heaven is like unto a man that is an householder which bringeth forth out of his treasure things new and old." All who are instructed in the Scriptures should draw forth old truths and new applications, adaptations to meet every need. What a storehouse of treasure has he who is well stocked with the bounty of the Book!

"Faith and Doubt"
July 8, 1934

In the fourteenth chapter of Matthew Jesus asks the sinking disciple Peter, as He rescues him while walking upon the waves, "O thou of little faith, wherefore didst thou doubt?"

It is true that Peter sank in his venture of faith but he walked further upon the water than any other mere man ever walked. He sank because he saw the wind boisterous and was afraid, that is he took his eyes off Jesus and fixed them on circumstances. Back of it all was doubt that crept in and upset the firmness of his faith.

The Christian life is a walking upon the waves toward Jesus. But so many believers hesitate to leave the boat, they put first this foot then that, into the water. There is nothing to fear if we walk toward Jesus and keep the eyes fixed upon Him. And even if our faith should momentarily yield to doubt, we may sink but we won't drown. For He is there to hear our cry and rescue us.

Doubt manifests itself in many forms. Some doubt whether they are saved. God's Word has given us definite assurances of salvation and to doubt our salvation after we have trusted Christ is simply to doubt God. We say we are doubting self but really we doubt God for salvation does not depend upon self but upon God. Such passages as Acts.

16:31, 2 Tim. 1:12, John 3:16, 36, and the whole book of First John as well as many other passages give us God's clear word of certainty. And if we are not certain that we ever trusted Christ truly for salvation, we can trust Him at any moment and be certain!

An old saint, who lay dying, moaned that in his feeble mental condition he had forgotten all the promises of God and could recall none of them. "But God has not forgotten," wisely suggested the old minister who sat beside him. How precious that, though we forget, God does not!

Some doubt the doctrines and teachings of the Word and find it hard to believe some of the Bible. There is much there which I cannot understand but none that I do not believe. I know that if I cannot understand a passage that does not mean that it cannot be understood. Doubt was the serpent's weapon in Eden. He raised a question: "Yea, hath God said?" In His temptation our Lord met the adversary with "Yea, God hath said!" There are too many question-mark Christians and not enough of the exclamation-point kind.

Many more are bothered, not so much with doubt of salvation or of the Scriptures, but practical doubt in every-day matters. Peter believed in Christ but it broke down here in a practical crisis. Theoretically we believe Rom. 8:28, reading it some pleasant summer afternoon under a shade tree in a hammock. But when trouble, sickness, death arrive, is our theoretical faith actual?

Peter took his eyes off Jesus. We must keep "looking unto Jesus" and "consider Him...lest we be wearied and faint in our minds." Doubt spoils the faith-life. We shift from Christ to circumstance. Like the Samaritan woman we argue that "the well is deep" (Jn. 4:11). Like Martha we reason, "he has been dead four days" (Jn. 11:39). Like the Emmaus disciples we reason that "this is the third day" (Lk. 24:21). Against all that comes our Lord's challenge: "Said I

"Faith and Doubt"

not unto thee, that if thou wouldest believe, thou shouldest see the glory of God?"

Believing is seeing.

"Walking the Waves Toward Jesus"
August 9, 1936

Peter is the only mere human who ever walked on water. Probably he did not go very far but he went farther than anyone else ever has gone.

It is a stormy night and the disciples in the boat are "tossed with waves, for the wind was contrary." Verily, we are in tempestuous times nowadays: the waves are boisterous, the wind against us. But Jesus is still walking the sea. Do not despair, however buffeted; in the fourth watch of your night He will come toward you.

The disciples are terrified when they see Jesus; they say, it is a spirit: they cry out with fear. How the old Book shows up the humanness of believers! It is a "spook"! Sometimes we do not know the Lord when He does come to our rescue.

Then comes the blessed reassurance: "Be of good cheer; it is I; be not afraid." No matter how dark the night, how nearly upset your frail bark, cheer up, the Lord is on the sea!

Peter speaks up: "Lord, if it be thou, bid me come unto thee on the water." He is throwing a challenge to the Lord. Yet I rather like his daring proposition. He is impetuous, venturesome, and it often gets him into trouble but there is nothing dull and commonplace about Simon Peter. He does not say, "Lord, if it be Thou, come to our aid" but "Let me come to Thee." He wants God to give him something to do, and God likes to give such men a dare. So Jesus says, "Come."

Peter walks some distance at least but his characteristic weakness shows up. "When he saw the wind boisterous, he was afraid." He got his mind on circumstances and when a believer looks away from Christ to circumstance, sink he must. He must cry for help and the Lord rescues him, saying "O thou of little faith, wherefore didst thou doubt?"

Are you alarmed in your boat and afraid to walk toward Jesus? You put first this foot, then that, into the water, "Yes, I know I should walk by faith and not by sight but it looks so dangerous. I shall not hold out, are you sure He will keep me?"

What if you do have a sinking spell! Suppose you do weaken out there and think of the wind! Jesus is looking at you! Better walk by faith a little way and have to cry "Lord, save me" than to live the smug, safe life of those who never step out on His promises! If you wait until you are sure that you never will sink you will never walk by faith. But you can be sure of this: If you walk toward Him and call to Him when your faith grows small, you may sink but you will not drown! If only we faltering souls could see that and live by it how we might tread triumphantly every stormy sea! He does not guarantee you that your faith will not falter, that you will not forget and begin to sink. But He has promised to lose no life committed to Him.

You are going through this world but once. Have you been up to now a poor, terrified doubter in a battered boat? Walk the waves toward Jesus! Friends may discourage you, the skeptical may laugh, smug and safe souls may rate you a crank, but resolve for yourself: "Live or die, sink or swim, I will take God at His Word, and Jesus at His challenge. I had rather sink a thousand times and have Him pull me up again than never to have stepped out on His promise."

As with Peter here, there will always be for those who

"Walking the Waves Toward Jesus"

dare a happy ending. Like him you will walk with the Lord on the waves; the wind will cease; and you and those in the ship–believers who would not dare–will be constrained to cry, "Of a truth thou art the Son of God!"

"Walking the Waves to Jesus"
October 27, 1935

After feeding the five thousand our Lord got away from the multitude eager to make Him king and retired to a mountain to pray alone. He knew the danger of the superficial enthusiasm of crowds. Again and again in His ministry we see such a reaction to the threat of popularity (Jn. 2:23-25; Lk. 14:25-35; Mk. 1:37; Jn. 6:22-26.) Today we measure men by the approval of the multitude but Jesus only had compassion upon them as sheep without a shepherd.

While He was at prayer the disciples were caught in a furious storm out on the sea. It must have been fearful to alarm seasoned fishermen. Our Lord once again proved His mastery over nature by an act which cannot possibly be explained away. He went to them walking on the waves. The storm-beset disciples, already terrified by the tempest, took Him to be a ghost. His answer, "Be of good cheer; it is I ; be not afraid" carries the answer to fear. Notice the negative, "Be not afraid" and the positive, "Be of good cheer" and between the two our Lord Himself, "It is I." He always changes negative to positive!

Impetuous Peter would walk to Jesus on the waves. He did not walk far but at least he walked farther than any other man has gone! He took his eyes off Jesus and fixed them on circumstances, saw the wind boisterous and was afraid, and he sank. It is always so when we fail to look unto Jesus.

But the Lord rescued him. Are you afraid by faith to walk the waves, first this foot, then that but we will not have the boat of self-security and commit ourselves to the walk of faith. We are afraid we may sink but we should remember that even though we should sink we will not drown! Peter sank but he did not drown. We have no business getting our eyes off Jesus and going down but if we do let us remember that He is out there with us and will rescue us.

Our Lord rebuked Peter's weak faith: "Oh thou of little faith, wherefore didst thou doubt?" We are not believing when we are doubting. What must He say to us today afraid to walk to Him in the smallest matters!

When He was received into the ship the wind ceased. Matthew tells us that they worshiped Him and Luke that they willingly received Him but Mark adds they were sore amazed and wondered for they considered not the miracle of the loaves and their heart was hardened. If they had rightly valued and appreciated the feeding of the five thousand they would have expected no less than His walking on the sea. We forget today what Christ has done and it lessens our expectation of what He can and will do. Our hearts are hardened! We have no right to censure these stupid disciples for we are even as they.

Coming to Gennesaret our Lord at once began to heal throngs again. "As many as touched Him were made perfectly whole." If only we believed might not a touch of Him Who bare our sicknesses and infirmities still work its wonders?

"Give Ye Them to Eat"
October 20, 1935

Three Gospels (Mt. 14:1-12; Mk. 6:14-29; Lk. 9:7-9) chronicle the death of John the Baptist. The rugged old prophet had condemned Herod's marriage to his brother's wife. The king admired the sturdy prophet "knowing that he was a just man and a holy" but he kept him in prison. A big banquet, a hilarious time and a dancing girl brought on plenty of trouble. Herod lost his head and John literally lost his, and many have lost their heads before and since that time because of a dancing girl. Having made a foolish vow, Herod must be a "good sport" and keep it. The world's code of principles is all awry, he had better broken the oath than add one sin to another. So the head of John the Baptist lies on the charger.

The sturdy old forerunner lived a hard life that few could have endured. Without family, his home the wilderness, he denounced in blazing terms the evils of his day. Kings and princes did not intimidate him and he paid for his devotion to truth with his life. What a rebuke to those who fancy the spiritual life of a soft, white-collared pursuit!

The feeding of the five thousand is the only miracle recorded in all four of the Gospels (Mt. 14:13-21; Mk. 6:30-46; Lk. 9:10-17; Jn. 6:1-15.) There is no explaining it away as some would do by making Christ's example an appeal to the generosity of the people who brought their food together and distributed it. Here our Lord is again Master of nature and this time He meets the age-old problem. "What shall we eat." The lad gave such as he had, the best he had, all he had, and little became much as is always the case when the Lord takes it over. He can do wonders with the smallest gifts fully surrendered.

John gives a different slant. Jesus asked Philip, "when shall we buy bread that these may eat?" In order to test him for "He Himself knew what He would do." Sometimes the Lord brings us to a crisis and seems to ask us, "Well, what are you going to do now?" and the situation looks hopeless. But remember that however impossible the case looks to you He always knows what to do if you will yield to His will He will work the wonder. Philip saw only the natural circumstances, "Two hundred pennyworth of bread is not sufficient." When God would use us to feed others let us not look at bare facts. Andrew mentioned the boy's loaves and fishes but added, "What are they among so many?" In the presence of the world's need your gifts, talents, abilities may appear pitiful but if you surrender them to Him He can feed the multitudes.

Notice that there was a surplus of twelve baskets full. God does nothing niggardly, parsimoniously. There is always overflowing abundance of blessing. so tremendous was the impression of this miracle that the crowd would make Jesus king by force. Ah, it was because they thought He could furnish bread and not for the Bread of Life that they would crown Him! Men ever desire a kingdom of outward prosperity but His kingdom is not of this world.

"Keep Thy Heart"
November 10, 1935

One is amazed at the Pharisees and scribes who could look over all the mighty works and teachings of our Lord and fasten upon such a petty matter as the fact that His disciples did not wash their hands, according to traditional regulations (Mt. 15:1-20; Mk. 7:1-23.) Yet we still have with us those who value set customs above the inner realities, to whom sacrifice is more important than mercy. Our Lord described both classes with His quotation from Isa. 29:13: "This people draweth nigh unto me with their mouth, and honoureth me with their lips; but their heart is far from me."

Jesus recognized a clean heart above clean hands. He reproved them for their "corban" custom by which they dedicated gifts to God and therefore escaped giving them to the needy. It was well to vow gifts to God but it had degenerated into a clever excuse for not helping the ones in need, a pretext for evading responsibility.

It is not what goeth into a man but what proceeds from him, his thoughts and acts which reveal his heart, these defile him. Out of the abundance of the heart the mouth speaketh. Therefore, "keep thy heart with all diligence for out of it are the issues of life."

Such teaching offended the Pharisees but Jesus said,

"Let them alone: they be blind leaders of the blind. And if the blind lead the blind, both shall fall into the ditch." It reminds us of the Old Testament statement: "Ephraim is joined to idols: let him alone" (Hos. 4:17.) Our Lord made no effort to rescue these Pharisees, He regarded them as hopelessly set against Him, they committed the sin against the Holy Ghost.

Well does formal and religious America need to ponder our Lord's position as to outward ritual and inward reality. Throughout the Word God cries against it, through Isaiah (1:11-17), Hosea (6:6), Amos (5:21-24.) Jesus followed the prophets with their own words, hurling them against an entrenched religiousness that could become excited over a slight disregard for precedent but could not see the truth of the Son of God.

Today sticklers for the niceties of tradition still strain out the gnat and swallow the camel, are careful to observe seasons and ordinances and minute church restrictions but their heart is far from God. Jesus would break a precedent and smash a tradition anytime to get at a needy life. Sabbath regulations were less important than a withered hand.

There are even Christians who have bordered on medieval asceticism by denying themselves wholesome and normal enjoyment and regulating each detail with meticulous care until they have fallen into the error of the Colossians, "Touch not, taste note, handle not." One is not more holy by being less human. It is the state of the heart that matters most for evil comes from within. It does no good to cleanse the hands with water if the heart has not be cleansed by the blood.

"As Thou Wilt"
November 17, 1935

Jesus' ministry in the coasts of Tyre and Sidon is marked by the wonderful story of the Syrophenician woman (Mat. 15:21-28; Mark 7:24-30). He had not planned a public ministry in these parts, but Mark tells us "He could not be hid." Neither can a true Christian be hidden, men will find him out.

This woman, outside the pale of His ministry to Israel, besought Him for her demonized daughter, but we read, "He answered her not a word." Prayer often meets such a Divine silence, but few of us press on to an answer as did this needy soul. Too often we take silence to mean refusal.

The disciples ask our Lord, it appears from what follows, to grant his request and send her away. These poor men, as with Bartimeus later, were continually trying to handle the cases that came to Jesus, but not in His way. He answers, "I am not sent but unto the lost sheep of the house of Israel," which indicates that they had meant for Him to grant her request to get rid of her. It is another clear declaration of His ministry to the Jew first. "He came unto His own and His own received Him not."

Not rebuffed at this, the woman beseeches Him, "Lord, help me," identifying herself with her daughter's need. Still stronger is the Lord's reply: "It is not meet to take the children's bread and to cast it to dogs." It is a severe answer. We pass over the sternness of our Lord in these soft, sentimental days. Had the woman come with less than genuine, importunate faith, this would have sent her away insulted, this calling the Jews "children" and the Gentiles "dogs." But our Lord uses the term for little household dogs and the woman catches the clue. "True, we may not have the bread, but surely we may share the crumbs." Here is humility and perseverance that will not be denied! It is he who is willing to take crumbs who receives bread.

Such faith draws from our Lord the gracious answer: "O woman, great is thy faith: be it unto thee as thou wilt." Notice, it is as thou wilt." There is a faith that desires and asks, but here faith goes further and wills. Jesus tells us (Mark 11:35) that whosoever shall command a mountain shall be moved and shall not doubt but believe, he shall have whatsoever he saith. Mind you, He does not say, "Whosoever shall ask God to move the mountain," but "Whosoever shall say unto this mountain, Be thou removed." Here is faith that dares to command. "Concerning the word of my hands, command ye me." (Isa. 45:11.)

Mark tells us that He said, "For this saying go thy way; the devil is gone out of thy daughter." Such faith always sends us on our way and as we go we are cleansed, as it was with the lepers (Luke 17:15). The woman went, Mark tells us, and found it even as He had said. So did the nobleman (Jn. 4:51). Oh how rare is the faith that takes Him at His word and goes on believing!

"Why Reason Ye?"
November 23, 1935

After the incident of the Syrophenician woman, Matthew (15:29-31) and Mark (7:31-37) record the healing of many lame, blind, dumb, maimed and many others. Mark singles out the healing of a deaf man with an impediment in his speech. Alas, all of us are deaf to heaven and only Jesus can loose our tongues in true testimony! He tried to avoid superficial sensationalism by charging that they tell no man but His fame spread.

Next He fed four thousand, an entirely different miracle from the feeding of the five thousand as Mark plainly tells us (8:19, 20). Not only can our Lord open our eyes and ears and loose our tongues but He feeds us with Himself, the bread of life.

Then the Pharisees and Sadducees came to Him seeking a sign. It was an unholy union of two Jewish groups at odds with each other but here united in common cause against the Lord. He answers with that mighty declaration that they can read the signs of the weather but cannot read the signs of the times. How true today! Men scan the daily weather forecast for an uncertain prediction but make light of the sure word of prophecy in the Bible lying on the table. These very days through which we now are passing are unmistakably foretold in the Old Book but when we preach them, men laugh at "excitable pre-millenialism."

Our Lord left these inquisitors with no sign, according to Mark, but with the sign of Jonas according to Matthew, the sign of the resurrection (Mt. 12:39-41.) Then He crossed the sea with His disciples who forgot to take bread along. On the other side He, with His mind still on the Pharisees and Sadducees, said, "Take heed and beware of the leaven of the Pharisees and of the Sadducees." The disciples, with their minds on the lack of bread, said, "It is because we have taken no bread." No wonder our Lord said, "O ye of little faith, why reason ye among yourselves, because ye have brought no bread?" Then He reminds them of the fact that He has just fed five thousand with a few loaves and fishes and that what He had in mind was the evil teaching of the Pharisees and Sadducees.

For us the application is plain. How stupid of these disciples to be worrying over the lack of bread when they had just seen our Lord feed thousands with a few loaves! Would Jesus be bothered over the lack of a little bread when He could work such wonders? Yet we today profess to believe in a miracle-working God who spreads tables in the wilderness and supplies meal in the barrel and then we reason among ourselves because we have no bread. We worry about daily needs, we gather in a huddle in our churches to devise plans to meet expenses, we forget the supernatural and become panicky in the face of a crisis. Theoretically we believe in a God Who supplies all our needs but when we find resources dwindling and an emergency on hand we reason among ourselves to meet the situation. A Christ Who could take a few loaves and feed multitudes is ready to prove His power in our individual lives and in our churches when we quit reasoning among ourselves and let Him work.

"Faith and Spiritual Stupidity"
July 15, 1934

Some critics have argued that the disciples could not possibly have been as stupid as they appear in Matt. 16:7. It was just after the feeding of the four thousand. Jesus had been interviewed by the Pharisees and Sadducees and they were on His mind. The disciples had forgotten to take bread on the boat by which He had left His enemies, and that was on their minds. So, when our Lord said, "Take heed and beware of the leaven of the Pharisees and of the Sadducees," one can understand how the disciples, with bread on their minds, could say, "It is because we have taken no bread."

Still it was stupid of them and our Lord says to them, "O ye of little faith, why reason ye among yourselves, because ye have brought no bread?" Gentile leaven was regarded unclean and since Jesus had pronounced Pharisees and Sadducees even lower than Gentiles, they thought He might be advising them to beware even of their bread. But our Lord reminds them of His miraculous feeding of the multitudes as if to say, "If I could do that would I be bothering now about the lack of bread?" Then He tells them that He has in mind the false doctrine of the Pharisees and Sadducees.

But how like many of us today were these weak disciples! They had seen the Lord feed multitudes miraculously but now against a practical difficulty they forgot all that and saw only immediate circumstance. So Christians today theoretically believe that Christ can work miracles, believe that God can supply all our needs, but when an actual problem looms they lapse back into fear and doubt and faithlessness. We have no bread today in more ways than one: like the man in Lk. 11 our friends come to us in their journey and we have nothing to set before them and we grow panicky. Preachers have no bread to feed the congregation, teachers to feed students, parents to feed children. But we need not grow worried like these disciples. We know the way to the Father's house where is abundant bread, loaves for every need.

How stupid we are, slow to believe our God! The mistake of these disciples went deep. They totally misunderstood what our Lord was speaking about. We reason among ourselves too much today. For the lack of faith we debate Scripture and miss its meaning a mile because we try to unravel it among ourselves. Faith unlocks the Word. It steps out upon what it does understand and the rest clears up. Scholarship never understand the Bible unless it goes in by the door of faith.

So everywhere we see Christians reasoning among themselves and worried over shortage of bread, physical as well as spiritual. How our Lord must say to us, "O ye of little faith, do ye not yet understand?" He is still able to prepare tables in the wilderness but we fall back upon our own devices in fear and trembling. We believe the promises in a way but when an actual crisis looms we grieve Him by our stupidity.

Churches huddle today in conference after conference reasoning over depleted resources and worried for the lack of break. But God's storehouse is as full as ever. It is our faith that has failed. We are not feeding the souls of men because we are grinding our own grist and men starve on husks; He Who fed the multitudes has still His ancient power.

"Thou Art the Christ"
December 1, 1935

Mark relates the gradual healing of a blind man by our Lord. First he saw men as trees walking, then after a second touch he saw clearly. Is it not a lesson that not all are healed instantly but that our Lord often uses a gradual process?

Three Gospels (Mt. 16:13-20; Mk. 8:27-30; Lk. 9:18-21) record Peter's confession of our Lord as the Christ, the Son of God. Men still differ about our Lord's first question: "Whom do men say that I am?" He is still one of the prophets or the great teacher or a great ideal. But He comes down to the individual with "Whom say ye that I am?" It is because of who He is that Christ is what He is. Many speak kindly of Him today who will not confess Him as Christ and Son of God.

Much argument has raged about our Lord's statement: "Upon this rock I will build my church." Of course, it has been made to mean Peter himself, a view utterly out of line with the Word for Peter never claimed to be more than an apostle and elder. It has been held that the church was built upon Peter as a type of redeemed humanity confessing Christ as Son of God. This would make the church rest upon man. Some hold that the church is built upon his confession but the church does not rest upon a creed or a doctrinal statement. It is more likely that our Lord meant by "this rock" Himself for Christ is the foundation of the church as Peter Himself says (1 Pt. 2:4-9.)

Against this church all the powers of hell shall not prevail. Then, our Lord gives to Peter the keys of the kingdom of heaven. Not the keys to heaven, nor to eternal life but to the kingdom in the sphere of Christian profession. It was Peter who opened the door of Christian opportunity to the Jews on the day of Pentecost (Acts 2:38-42) and to the Gentiles in the house of Cornelius (Acts 10:34-46.) But let us remember that Peter was not infallible for he himself tried to close the very door which he opened (Gal. 2:11-18.)

The power of binding and loosing was not authority to decide the eternal destinies of souls but authority to pass upon matters of discipline and doctrinal and moral issues. A rabbi received at ordination authority to decide upon what was lawful and unlawful. That which was allowed as lawful was said to be "loosed" and that which was unlawful was "bound." This is the terminology our Lord used.

It is evident that we have here a delegated authority which the church today is failing to use. Of course it must be used only under the Spirit's guidelines and it is there we fail because we are so little under the Spirit that when we undertake these matters we decide and act mainly in the strength of the flesh. The thought is well brought out in John 20:22-23, where authority to retain or remit sins is given but it is first prefaced by the breathing of the Holy Ghost. Unless the Spirit empowers and directs we have no true authority and can only make matters worse.

"This is My Beloved Son"
December 8, 1935

Right after his God-revealed confession Peter undertakes to rebuke the Lord Jesus. Within the range of a few verses He falls from the mountain peaks of confession to the swamps of contradiction. From a rock he changes to a stumbling block. A few moments and he who spoke from God is told he savors not the things of God but of men.

Jesus next laid down the terms of discipleship in self-denial, cross-bearing and obedience. There is a difference between a believer and a disciple. Not every believer is a good disciple. He gives us the paradox of Christian experience: he who loses his life for Christ's sake saves it. To gain the world and lose the soul is man's worst bargain. At the judgment we are to be rewarded according to works.

The statement, "There be some standing here which shall not taste of death, till they see the Son of man coming in His kingdom," is fulfilled in the transfiguration which immediately followed (Mt. 17:1-3; Mk. 9:2-13; Lk. 9:28-36). The whole scene is a miniature picture of Christ reigning in His future kingdom. He is the centre of it all. Moses represents dead saints resurrected and Elijah, the lying saints caught up at the rapture. Peter, James and John represent Israel while the multitude at the foot of the mountain represent the nations to be brought into the kingdom after it is established over Israel. Peter himself speaks of the profound significance of this occasion (2 Pt. 1:10-19).

Impulsive Peter wanted to catch the glory and house it and stay on the mountain top but there is work to be done in the valley and he must go down to meet human need. The heavenly voice bears testimony to the beloved Son, as at the baptism of our Lord, and when the glory passes, they see Jesus only. We must not fix upon our rapturous experiences as the norm of our Christian lives. Mountain-top experiences come and go but Christ remains.

Observe also that after such a glorious experience Jesus bids them "Arise and be not afraid." After our visions and revelations we are to arise. The strength that comes through them must be expended on the multitude at the foot of the mountain. Mountain-top hours are not for purely personal enjoyment. They are to brace us for practical service ahead.

The disciples ask about Elijah who is to come (Mal. 4:5,6). Malachi's prediction had already been fulfilled in John the Baptist, but there is a greater fulfillment ahead when he comes as one of the two witnesses in Rev. 11. Two separate comings are clearly taught, the first in the person of John the Baptist but another yet future.

Luke says, "And when the voice was past, Jesus was found alone." We have our great days, when voices from heaven speak to the soul. But Jesus Himself abides when the vision fades and no voice is heard. Look not to voice and vision but unto Him Who remains the same.

"As a Little Child"
December 22, 1935

Three Gospels (Mt. 18:1-4; Mk. 9:33-50; Lk. 9:46-50) record the touching incident of our Lord and the little children. The disciples had been disputing to who should be greatest in His kingdom. Our Lord upsets all prevailing standards by putting a child in the midst. We adults who like to act as though wisdom would die with us might have found it more comfortable to our pride if Christ had used a rabbi, a scholar, some "successful" man for His model but He commands us to be converted and childlike.

Most of us are like children but like the other group our Lord described in Mt. 11:16-19, we are childish rather than childlike. He would have us be simple in faith, in life, in spirit, in service, nothing affected or forced. And woe unto him who offends a child or a young believer! Notice what a stern term our Lord used, "better that a millstone be hanged around his neck and he be cast into the sea."

He commands us to cut off hand or foot if they offend us–anything that cripples our Christian experience, however precious. He tells us that the children have their guardian angels in the presence of God just as all saints have ministering spirits (Heb. 1:14). And He came to seek and to save the lost, going as a good shepherd after the sheep that is lost.

In speaking of hell the Lord uses most awful terms,

"where the worm dieth not and the fire is not quenched." Some who want to hear love preached all the time and who do not reconcile hell with the meek and lowly Jesus should remember that He had more to say about hell than anyone else in the Bible. Here He has in mind the valley of Hinom where the worm worked in the putrefaction of decaying bodies and where the smoke continually ascended. The worm does not die in hell because the putrefaction never ceases.

The disciples also complain in this passage about some one who was casting out devils in Christ's name but who was following with them. Our Lord's rebuke, "Forbid him not, for he that is not for us is against us," ought to govern us more today that it does. We censure other disciples who are not of us but if they do the work and in His Name, we should esteem them as brothers and not as competitors. It is deplorable that the ranks of true Christian, few enough at most, should be divided by rank jealousies and petty criticisms.

So here is a double warning, against offending weak Christians and children on the one hand, and against censuring others who work in His Name on the other. Rather we are to have salt in ourselves and have peace one with another. Too many of us are "fresh" Christians, we must be seasoned and salted so that our speech may be seasoned with salt, and often that takes fiery trial and suffering. It is not easy for the childish to become childlike.

"The Unmerciful Servant"
December 29, 1935

After the incident of the little children Matthew records further teaching of our Lord upon the same occasion (Mt. 18:15-35). He gives us true procedure with an offending brother in the church. Strange that we should overlook such plain instruction in our church discipline nowadays! The offended party is to go to the offender alone; if reconciliation cannot be effected that way, two or three others are to be taken along the second time; if that fails the church is to act and if he hear not the church, he is to be treated as an heathen and a publican, not despised but as one outside the fold.

Then follows the word of authority about binding and loosing which we considered in the study of Peter's confession. Next is the promise that where two agreed as touching anything they shall ask, it is granted of the Father, and that where two or three gather in His Name, He is there. Another glorious check we fail to cash! We roll it under our tongues as a precious promise but it is not a motto for the wall but an endorsed check to present at the Bank of Heaven.

Peter asks about forgiveness and our Lord tells the story of the unmerciful servant who, himself forgiven of a great debt, chokes a fellow servant who owes but a mite. We believers are forgiven of an incalculable debt against God since "Jesus paid it all." Shall we not freely forgive again and again those who wrong us? Of course, this is primarily Kingdom teaching and does not mean that we are lost if we do not forgive others. Rather we are bidden to forgive one another "even as God for Christ's sake hath forgiven us." The absence of a forgiving spirit shows that the professing believer does not have the Spirit of Christ and is none of His.

Going back, it is interesting to note the place our Lord claims for Himself in the promise that where two or three gather in His Name He is there. If He were not the Son of God, what comfort would there be in knowing He was there when we prayed? How precious to know that He Himself intercedes as our Advocate before the Father!

This Christ is with us when we pray and if we hold malice and will not forgive He knows it. Peter of course was still on Jewish ground for the fuller light of grace had not yet liberated him. The rabbis taught that trespass should be forgiven three times. Peter no doubt congratulated himself that he would be willing to make it seven. But in the spirit there is no limit to forgiveness nor any Christian exercise. When we set a limit to how much we will forgive or to any such matter we lapse back into legalism. Our Lord answered Peter in kingdom terms but today we must remember that the reason for our forgiving others is not that we may be forgiven but because we are forgiven.

"Occupy Till I Come"
June 14, 1936

Jesus entered Jerusalem as the Messiah (Mt. 21:1-11; Mk. 11:1-11; Lk. 19:26-44; Jn. 12:12-19). He dropped all reserve and for a brief time assumed His position publicly as the long-expected One Who should come. He entered as King; later He acted as Prophet and Priest. He fulfilled prophecy and entered in the way predicted (Zech. 9:9). But He was refused. However, one day, He will enter Jerusalem as King and will reign. He knew upon this entry that He would be rejected and that the bitter way of the Cross lay just ahead. Before He can reign as triumphant King He must die as suffering Servant.

Luke records His weeping over the city. Their eyes were blinded, their hearts hardened. What misery the years have brought upon the city that refused Him! His prophecy that the enemies should cast a trench about Jerusalem and lay it even with the ground and not leave one stone upon another, was literally fulfilled.

They did not realize that their day of visitation was upon them. They had their chance and did not know it. Is it not so with men today? Christ calls us and we do not heed the Spirit's pleading. One day He will come in judgment. Ah, that we knew the things which belong unto our peace! Pharasaism stands by and scoffs at the believer's joy.

Sadduccism criticizes in its skepticism. A wild world hurtles onward to ruin. But He will come again to reign and woe unto His enemies in that day!

Jesus proceeded to cleanse the temple. After He enters the temple of the heart He cleanses away all that offends. He made a rugged use of force. As He worked He quoted Scripture (Isa. 56:7; Jer. 7:11). To the surprised and displeased Pharisees He quoted more (Ps. 8:2). There are still those stilted an sanctimonious souls who resent joy in God's house. The hallelujahs and hosannas have gone from our churches.

The fig tree which Christ condemned to unfruitfulness is a type of the Jewish nation having only the leaves of the external religiousness but no spiritual reality. Jesus condemns symbolically the Jewish nation and that has been fulfilled. The fig tree is beginning to put forth leaves nowadays in the revival of Jewry in its rehabilitation of Palestine. This is a clear sign that the end draws nigh (Mt. 24:32-33).

The fig tree incident is also an illustration on the power of faith. Peter seemed surprised that the tree had actually withered. He might have known it would when Jesus had said so! Is not that like our faith which asks but really doesn't expect to see things happen? The faith of God (Mk. 11:22) orders the mountain to move and then expects to see it move! Our prayers fail because we ask and then do not believe we have what we ask. We demand to see but faith takes without seeing and believes it has what it asked.

But the Lord also added here that we need not pray with an unforgiving spirit and expect to receive. Of course, under grace we forgive because we are forgiven but an unforgiving spirit breaks our fellowship and those out of fellowship cannot pray and receive because their hearts condemn them.

Jesus enters the heart as King and cleanses it as Priest. Is your heart a den of thieves?

"By What Authority"
June 21, 1936

He Who spake as one having authority and not as the scribes was challenged by the scribes as to that authority (Mt. 21:23-27). Our Lord met question with question by asking of them whether John's baptism was from heaven or of men. John had recognized Jesus and to recognize John therefore was to recognize Christ. To discredit John would be dangerous for the people believed in him. It was a Master stroke that utterly defeated the questioners.

Our Lord followed that by the parable of the two sons. The one who offered to go but did not is the prominent Jew who professed religion but did not receive Christ the other is the publican and sinner who made no profession but did receive the Light. This is clear from Jesus' declaration: "The publican and harlots go into the kingdom of God before you."

This does not teach that it is better to make no profession at all, just obey. Remember that John the Baptist is the topic, as verse 32 of Mt. 21 shows. The Pharisees had gloried in the Law and professed to follow it. Yet John was directly in the line of the Scriptures as the forerunner who was to come. They had refused him while the publicans and harlots who had not kept the law had accepted John's message and entered the kingdom.

Our Lord gave next the parable of the wicked husbandman in which He made clear claim to be the Son of God. God, the Husbandman, sends His servants, the prophets, to gather fruit of Israel. When they are rejected He sends His Son. Then came the judgment of God in the destruction of Jerusalem while the vineyard is let out to others, ministers and the church now standing by faith while Israel is cut off.

Jesus quotes Ps. 118:22 as applied to Himself: "The Stone which the builders, the same is become the head of the corner, this is the Lord's doing, and it is marvelous in our eyes." Christ is become the chief cornerstone. Gentiles have succeeded to the privilege once enjoyed of the Jew. But we are not to be high-minded but fear, lest we also be cut off (Rom. 11:13-25).

"Whosoever shall fall on this stone shall be broken: but on whomsoever it shall fall, it will grind him to powder." Those who fall upon Christ in repentance and conversion are broken in spirit but woe unto him upon whom Christ falls in judgment!

The parable of the marriage of the king's son (Mt. 22:1-14) pictures a king, God, making a marriage for His Son, Christ, (marriage of Christ and the church begun here and perfected hereafter, 2 Cor. 11:1, Rev. 21:2). He sent His servants from Moses to John to call them that were bidden, the Jews. Other servants, the early church, went forth inviting but they were rejected and persecuted. Then came the Roman armies and destroyed Jerusalem. Now all who can be found, Gentiles of every walk, are invited, both bad and good. One man comes not dressed in the true garment which is the righteousness of Christ Himself. Having form of godliness but no power, he is cast into outer darkness. Many are called but few are chosen, and the chosen are they who wear the garments provided by the King.

"What Think Ye of Christ?"
June 28, 1936

As the enemies of our Lord seek to entrap Him, it is wonderful to watch His conduct and His replies. The Pharisees tried to snare Him on the question of tribute but He answers: "Render therefore unto Caesar the things which are Caesar's; and unto God the things that are God's." The state has its claims but we never must give it that allegiance which belongs only to God.

Next they asked Him concerning the resurrection, whose wife should she be who had married seven. Our Lord replies, laying down the basis of error: "Ye do err, not knowing the Scriptures, nor the power of God." So many believers today either do not study the Bible and depend too much upon experience or else they read the Bible and do not heed what they read so do not know the power of God.

He declares that earthly conditions and relationships do not prevail hereafter. Then God said, I AM the God of Abraham, of Isaac and Jacob," not "I was..." In His sight all live; He does not speak of them as having been. Besides, God had made promises to these patriarchs which necessitated resurrection if they were to be realized (Gen. 17:8, 28:13; Heb. 11:13).

A scribe asks which is the great commandment and our Lord quotes from the Old Testament (Dt. 6:5; Lev. 19:18) the two commandments of love for God and one's neighbor, upon which hang all the others. Certainly if you keep the first, you will keep the first five of the ten commandments and if you keep the second, you will keep the second five.

Now notice the grand climax. Our Lord Himself propound the next question: "What think ye of Christ? Whose Son is He?" It is as though He said, "All these questions you have asked are secondary. What about Myself? That is the supreme issue." It was the supreme matter then. It is today. After that, they asked Him no more questions. There are no more questions after that! For Jesus Christ is the last word and when you stubbornly refuse Him as did these, there is nothing more to be said. They made Him to be only David's Son but He refuted it from the Scriptures.

Then he turned in the twenty-third chapter of Matthew to the most flaming condemnation of Pharasaism of His entire ministry. The charges He brings are terrific. They do not practice what they preach. They love clerical show and high places at conventions and lofty titles. They obstruct the conversion of others. They cheat the poor and pray long prayers. They encouraged dishonesty. They see little faults in others and commit great sins themselves. They are hypocrites, righteous without and vile within, whitewashed, not washed white. They had killed the great prophets of the past. They are snakes, sure for hell.

No more awful condemnation of any group of people has ever been delivered. It is noteworthy that our Lord never spoke of–or to the Pharisees except in judgment for they were blind leaders of the blind and His attitude was, "Let them alone." Some people cannot be won, they can only be let alone.

From this fiery message Jesus turns to lament over Jerusalem. Notice the responsibility is theirs, "and ye would not." Jerusalem must be desolate until Israel receives her long-rejected Messiah.

"The Last Supper"
July 12, 1936

In the twenty-fifth chapter of Matthew, our Lord, following His prophecy in the twenty-fourth gives the parable of the 10 virgins. The foolish virgins were unprepared, had only a superficial experience that soon gave out. The wise cannot divide at the last day with the unprepared. Many fanciful and overdrawn interpretations of this parable overlook its simple lesson of proper preparation of the Lord's return.

The talents represent the various degrees of endowments and abilities which God gives us with which we are to occupy till He comes. The first two men made a short report; the man who had gained nothing made the longest speech! He had not squandered his gift, mind you; but he had not used it. "I was afraid" is the secret of many lost lives.

The Lord's account of the judgement in this same chapter is held by some to be the judgment of nations for their treatment of Israel, by others to be the judgment of professing Christians whose faith does not issue in works. Notice that the wicked are cursed by not "of my Father" as the righteous were blessed; and hell is prepared for the devil and his angels, but those who prefer his company here must keep it here-after.

Judas, the son of perdition, begins his work of betrayal. Although it was part of God's plan, still Judas was personally responsible. It is interesting to note how our Lord told them to follow the man with the pitcher of water. It seems strange guidance but shows that the tiniest detail is known ahead and all fits together in His plan.

The supper is an ordinance setting forth our Lord's death till He come. It shows Him as the Passover Lamb Whose blood must be applied to our hearts but it also shows Him as the Bread of Life. This truth is often overlooked. The Passover must be followed by the feast of unleavened bread. We see the blood but forget the bread. The life which begins with the blood applied must be continued by the Bread appropriated. "Except ye eat the flesh of the Son of man, and drink His blood, ye have no life in you" (John 6:38).

Following the supper our Lord set forth a very practical lesson in humility (John 13:1-39). What a wonderful contrast here: "Jesus, knowing that the Father had given all things into His hands, and that He was come from God, and went to God...washed feet." He could come down from magnificence to mentality! Some of us want to stay on the mountain top: we do not know the technique of the towel. Peter must have had this incident in mind when later he wrote, "Put on the apron of humility" (1 Pt. 5:5).

We read that Judas went out "and it was night" (verse 30). It is always night when a soul goes away from Jesus. Then our Lord gives his commandment of love. This is the mark of discipleship, that we love one another.

Simon Peter wanted to follow Jesus now but was told he should follow afterwards. That "afterwards" is very significant. Peter followed first from Galilee in much self-sufficiency; he had to come to the end of himself before, as Tiberias, he reached the second "follow me." The first time he forsook his nets: the second time he forsook himself. We cannot truly follow our Lord until "afterwards," after we have been broken in self and have come to Tiberias.

"Where Are You at Calvary?"
July 26, 1936

At the trial of our Lord, Peter warning at the enemies fire denies his Master. Beware of warming at the devil's fire. Jesus answers the priest's clear question, "Tell us whether thou be the Christ, the Son of God," with an unmistakable affirmative and prophesies His return. Judas returns the blood-money and hangs himself. He purchased his own graveyard with the proceeds of his iniquity. Trade with the devil and you buy a graveyard.

Pilate faced three alternatives: Cynicism or Christ; "What is truth?" Christ is the Answer to cynicism. He faced criminality or Christ in the choice between Barabas and the Lord. Christ is the answer to criminality's problem. And Pilate faced the issue of Caesar or Christ. And every one of us faces the one supreme question, Shall we crown or crucify Jesus?

It seems that God so arranged it that every type should be represented at the cross. If you look closely you will soon recognize your crowd. There were the soldiers who only administered the wounds which all the sin of all the world caused. They sat and watched Him and they gambled for His robe and so do men today idly face Calvary and gamble away their Gospel opportunity. If you are not a soldier of the cross, you are a soldier at the cross.

There were the passers-by who wagged their heads. It is

fashionable to pass Calvary wagging the head. They misquoted His claims, they minimized His death, they mocked His Deity. So men today see no need for Calvary.

Next were the chief priests, scribes and elders. No group of men has behaved worse at the cross than the religionists. Today there are no worse enemies of Christ than those hypocrites whose names are on church books, who work in church, read the Bible, pray in public, give money to church, but who merely draw near with their mouths and honor with their lips while their hearts are far from God.

Then, there were the people who merely stood beholding. They just looked on and did nothing. But all that anyone need to do to be lost is just...nothing. "How shall we escape if we NEGLECT so great salvation?" They smote their breasts and returned terrified. The publican in the temple smote his breast and went home justified because he truly repented.

The centurion went further. He feared greatly. He confessed that Christ was righteous; he called Him the Son and God; he glorified God. Yet one may do all this and be lost.

It is not wonderful that the one who got most out of that awful day was the lowest character of them all, the repentant thief. The first person to enter Paradise after our Lord was a thief! But is it not in keeping with the whole tenor of the Gospel of God hath chosen the base and despised and the ones who have profited most are those who have come without one plea His shed blood.

One other group remains, those who loved Him. We sing, "O, How I Love Jesus," but do we love Him crucified and do we love the old rugged cross?

After all, there are only two classes at the cross: those who rest upon the work He accomplished there for our redemption; and those who reject the provisions of His love. Where are you at Calvary?

"He is Risen"
August 2, 1936

The appearances of our Lord have been arranged from the different accounts in many ways. First, the women came to the tomb and saw the angel (Mt. 28:1-2). They announced the resurrection to the disciples. Peter and John came to the tomb and saw the linen clothes there. Our Lord appeared to Mary in the garden (John 20:11-18) and to the women (Mt. 28:9,10).

Precious is the story of the walk to Emmaus (Luke 24:13-35). These disciples were half-believing and half-doubting because "their eyes were holden" in more ways than one. Is Christ a veiled figure with you? Must He say, "Have I been with you so long time, yet hast thou not known me?" They were "slow of heart to believe all the prophets have spoken." Better slow of head to understand than slow of heart to believe! They did not understand about His first coming; today men do not believe concerning His return.

In this chapter Jesus opens the Scriptures, opens their eyes, opens their understanding. Always it must begin with the Word for "faith cometh by hearing and hearing by the word of God." When the Scriptures truly are opened, the Spirit will produce holy heartburn as He did here. And nothing is more needed today than a heartburn that all the dopes of sin and sedatives of Satan cannot relieve.

These disciples asked the Lord to abide with them and He made Himself known in breaking of bread. Often we look for some spectacular revelation when He would manifest Himself in the simple and humble way. They went back the seven miles to Jerusalem to tell of their experience. Our feet are not tired when we have seen the Lord! And as they testified He appeared again! He does reappear in testimony!

Our Lord appeared to Peter (Lk. 24:34). Peter had collapsed miserably and our Lord doubtless was preparing him for the great meeting at Tiberias. Meanwhile He appeared to the 10 disciples (Lk. 24:36), to the 11 (Mk. 16:14), to the disciples with Thomas present (John 20:26-29). Here is a precious lesson for us: We often wish we might see the Lord as did Thomas but to ask that would be asking a smaller blessing than to believe without seeing!

In John 21 our Lord appears to the disciples at Tiberias. Their own fishing expedition was futile until Christ appeared and gave orders. He then deals with Peter who has been reduced to his right size. Notice that our Lord does not call him Cephas or Peter, but only "Simon, son of Jonas." There is nothing of the rock about him now. He is broken in self and now he is commissioned to feed others. It is only when we have been centered that we can strengthen the brethren (Lk. 22:32).

Then the Lord appears to the 11 on the mountain with the great commission (Mt. 28:16-20). We are not only to teach the things commanded but to teach them to observe the things commanded. The "go" carries the "lo" of His presence.

Mark, Luke and Acts record the ascension, He Who went away is to return in like manner. It is tragic that this clear promise (Acts 1:11) has been ignored or so mistaught that few today are moved with the eager expectation of His personal return. If this fired us instead of the impossible dream of world conversion things would be different.

"He is Risen"

Meanwhile we are to occupy till He come. He is not a mere memory but living still and the Spirit within makes Him real to the believer as He is allowed to have His way.

"Our Marching Orders"
April 9, 1939

The great commission (Mt. 28:16-20) is our Lord's marching orders to believers. It was a mountain-top experience which is always a good thing if we carry the vision into the valley. We read that they gathered where Jesus had appointed them. We shall never meet Him nor get His instructions until we are in the place of his will, the place where He has asked us to be.

I read next that they saw Him. We shall see Him when we get into the place of His appointment. There can be no real service until first we have seen Him. "They looked unto Him and were brightened and their faces were not ashamed." "Then were the disciples glad when they saw the Lord." We see men, causes, challenges, but not the Lord. Isaiah saw the Lord and then was ready to go where God would send him. Paul saw the Lord, then asked, "What wilt thou have me to do?"

Next, they worshiped Jesus. We will worship Him if we really see Him. Thomas cried, "My Lord and my God" and Jesus did not reprove him for worshiping Him. Christian testimony and service are based on the worship of Christ as Lord, not upon admiration of Him as a teacher.

"But some doubted." Yet our Lord did not send them away because they doubted. "A bruised reed He will not break." These witnesses all grew strong and fearless and our Lord knew they would. It is not well to send John Mark home on his first offense.

Jesus said first, "All power is given unto me in heaven and in earth." He shows us first His resources, the power that is back of His orders. In Mat. 11:27,18, He says in effect, "All things are mine, Come." In John 17:2,3, He says, All power is mine, believe. Here it is, "All power is mine, go." We often flinch before our task but we need to remember Who is back of us. He is with us as He also says here but first He is back of us.

"Go ye therefore." We build churches today and wait for the people to come. Here we are bidden to go after them in the highways and hedges. Too many churches are glorified clubs that have forgotten about the shepherd seeking the sheep.

"Disciple all nations." Soul-fishing is the Christian's business. We are not to uplift, reform, cultivate them, but bring them to know the Lord. We have forgotten our commission and are out proselyting, calling the righteous to repentance, instead of bringing men to Christ.

Then we are to baptize them into the name of the Father, Son and Holy Ghost. Notice, disciplining and baptizing go together and we have no business separating them. In Acts, baptism immediately followed conversion. There was no thought of using ones opinion about being baptized, it was the very next step. At Pentecost, in Samaria, in the case of the eunuch, Cornelius, Lydia, the jailer, they obeyed at once.

"Teaching them to observe all things whatsoever I have commanded you." Not just to know them but to observe them. We have neither learned nor taught a Bible truth until we have observed it, put it into practice. As preachers and teachers we should, like lawyers, strive for a verdict and seek to bring to action.

Our Lord concludes with a promise to be with us always

"Our Marching Orders"

even unto the end of the age. He Who has all power is to be with us all the days, the good and bad, the sunshiny and the shadowy.

"The Keys of Christ"
April 8, 1934

In Mt. 28:18 the Lord Jesus Christ says, "All power is given unto me in heaven and in earth." With all that authority back of Him, it is interesting to notice the keys which God's Word says are His.

In Rev. 3:7 we read: "these things saith He that is holy, He that is true, He that hath the key of David, He that openeth, and no man shutteth; and shutteth, and no man openeth." The reference to the key of David carries us back to Isa. 22:22 where the Lord declares through Isaiah that the Shebna, an unworthy court favorite and treasurer, shall be displaced by God's servant Eliakim who shall bear the key of the house of David upon his shoulder. The prophecy is prophetic of Christ, Who is the true heir to the house of David and will one day reign over a redeemed and restored Israel. Isa. 9:6 tells us that the government shall be upon His shoulder.

The Lord Jesus Christ also, in this connection, carries the keys to the storehouse of Divine truth. "All things are delivered unto me of my Father" (Mt. 11:27). God's riches in glory are by Christ Jesus (Phil. 4:19) and only through Christ can we lay hold upon them.

Our Lord also carries the key to doors of Christian service. Paul spoke of opportunities for service as open doors (1 Cor. 16:9; 2 Cor. 2:12). When Christ opens a door and calls us to go in no man can shut that door, no one can prevent us. Men discouraged D.L. Moody but God had set before him an open door and he went in. Conversely, we must be careful not to try to open doors God has shut, and force ourselves where He does not direct. Paul knew the experience of shut doors also as in Acts 16:7.

In Mt. 16:19 the Lord Jesus Christ tells Peter: "And I will give unto thee the keys of the kingdom of heaven: and whatsoever thou shalt bind on earth shall be bound in heaven: and whatsoever thou shalt lose on earth shall be loosed in heaven." Not the keys to the church, nor the keys to eternity, but the privilege to open the door of the kingdom to the world is here meant. Peter exercised this privilege by opening the door to the Jews at Pentecost and to the Gentiles in the house of Cornelius. The "binding and loosing" in this passage combined with Mt. 18:15-19 is simply the delegation to the disciples of the powers of church discipline and does not mean authority to decide upon any soul's salvation. See also John 20:23.

In Rev. 1:18 our Lord declares that He has the keys of hell and death. He has conquered death and will eventually destroy it (1 Cor. 15:26). Death and hell ultimately are to be cast into the lake of fire (Rev. 20:14). The lake of fire is the final hell for sinners, the Gehenna of Jesus' messages (Mt. 11:23, etc.). Hell in Rev. 1:18 refers to hades the place where the spirits of the dead go. Hades is not to be identified with the final hell for then Christ would have been in that hell before His resurrection (Acts 2:25-31). Death is the condition of the body without the spirit. Hades is the condition of the spirit without the body. The key of both are with Him. He has the power to join body and spirit for their final destiny which He will exercise in the resurrection of the righteous (1 Thes. 4:13-18) and at the judgment of the Great White Throne (Rev. 20:11-15).

PART TWO

REFLECTIONS ON THE GOSPEL OF MARK

"A Prophet in His Own Country"
April 28, 1935

After John was cast into prison, our Lord came and dwelt in Capernaum, thus fulfilling Isa. 9:1,2 and 42:6,7. Mark tells us (1:14,15) that He came into Galilee saying, "The time is fulfilled, and the kingdom of God is at hand; repent ye and believe the Gospel." Luke tells us that He came to Galilee "in the power of the spirit." At Nazareth, His own home town, He went into the synagogue on the Sabbath day "as His custom was." It reminds us of Paul entering the synagogue of the Jews in Thessalonica "as his manner was." It is not the custom or manner of many nowadays, even many Christians to follow this example.

Anyone might address the congregation so our Lord stood up to read. He took His text from Isa. 61:1,2: "The Spirit of the Lord is upon me, because He hath anointed me to heal the broken-hearted, to preach deliverance to the captives, and recovering of sight to the blind, to set at liberty them that are bruised, to preach the acceptable year of the Lord." It is significant that He did not read the next statement from Isaiah, "and the day of vengeance of our God." This has to do with judgment and that will follow when Messiah comes. His message then was one of grace. Following this reading our Lord made a clear claim of Messiahship: "This day is this scripture fulfilled in your ears." But He knew they would not receive Him and He declared that truth proven so many times since that no prophet is accepted in his own country.

No doubt they were saying to Him in thought at least, "Why don't you do the wonders here you did at Capernaum?" Our Lord then refers to Elijah and Elisha who had the same experience, were not appreciated at home but did their greatest work among strangers. Here is a truth seldom mentioned today except to emphasize its exceptions. One hears occasionally, "So-and-so has proven an exception to the proverb about a prophet in his own country." But there is no doubt that preachers will fare better to go to new fields rather than settle where all the neighbors know them by the first name. Familiarity does breed contempt and a stranger from somewhere else with a poorer message will be received far better than home-talent with much to say. Perhaps it ought not be so but it is.

It would seem to follow as an inevitable corollary that even after they have settled in new fields it is not well for the average minister at least to be a hall-fellow-well-met on too many fish-frys and parlor get-togethers. People either look up to a preacher or down on him and too much back-slapping and regular fellow tactics add little to his power on Sunday. He will be called cranky anyway by some people, no matter what he does, so it is well to stay apart even too much and have the respect of those who might pick weak spots in his armor in too much gadding around.

The Lord Jesus Christ found He could do no mighty works where He had grown up. The applications of the proverb He stated should be more thoughtfully pondered today. None knew men so well as He and any principle He proved true can scarcely be overruled by you and me.

"Follow Me"
May 5, 1935

The call of the fishermen disciples by the sea (Mt. 4:18-22; Mk. 1:16-20) was really a second call, a call to service. Peter, Andrew and John were already disciples, having followed Christ as recorded in John 1:35-51. Notice that our Lord uses the same figure for their new work as the work they had been following "fishers of men." The Lord exalts and spiritualizes our work, transforms it into a heavenly calling. Here certainly is a call to soul-winning, a vocation not popular with many Christians. Some, falling back upon predestination, argue that God will convict and save those whom He chooses. That is true but one of the means He uses to convict the unsaved is the ministry of a personal worker.

The disciples followed "straightway" which implies that much still must be learned. Peter followed in much self-will and had to be humbled and broken in self before he could respond to the later "follow me" of Tiberias (John 21:19.) The two "follow me's" in his life are full of meaning for us, it is not every one who has followed from Galilee who will follow from Tiberias.

In Lk. 5:1-11 we have an incident probably parallel to this call by Galilee. After teaching in Peter's boat our Lord ordered them to launch into the deep and let down their nets for a drought. "For a drought," mind you, He expected results. Our Lord often orders us into deep water and after we have toiled all night in vain. Notice the "nevertheless" in Peter's reply, "We have taken nothing; nevertheless at Thy Word." We must come to the end of self, our own striving and then obey His Word. From "we" to "Thy" is transition for the Christian fisherman that never fails of results.

The results were overwhelming. Where they had failed all night they made their greatest catch. We have come today to where we expect little when we fish for souls. Much striving without our Lord has produced nothing and we neither hear nor heed His command. He Himself is not in the boat, that is the trouble. We have improved nets and standard instructions and good intentions but the nets are not filled. We are not working in His fellowship and at His Word.

Peter was convicted at the wonder of the catch and fell at the Lord's knees confessing his sinfulness. True success does not elate us with ourselves but convicts us of our sinfulness. Our Lord's reply shows that He meant to join the lesson taught there with spiritual soul-winning; "Fear not; from henceforth thou shalt catch men."

Meager results among Christians and churches are excused today with many flimsy arguments: we need not expect great revivals, we are told; it is the last days and as in the days of Noah. To save our faces and keep the appearances going children are graded into church from the Sunday schools. The real trouble is, we are toiling in our own strength, the Lord is not in the boat and we are not obeying His Word. Christians and churches venture on campaigns and programs of their own, the Lord is left out and His instructions are ignored.

If we met these conditions, once more the nets would fill, we should overcome at his feet, and He would commission us afresh to fishing for men.

"The Fever Cure"
May 14, 1939

In Mark 1:29-31, we have the terse, simple account of the healing of Peter's wife's mother. From the synagogue, the Lord Jesus enters Simon's home. Simon's mother-in-law is sick of a fever. They tell Jesus about her. He takes her by the hand, the fever leaves her. She arises and ministers unto them.

We live in a world sick of a fever. No word can describe the present international condition better than "feverish." Business is in a fever. Religion the world over is in a fever. We individuals live in a fever. Life may be spelled in three words, "Hurry, Worry, Bury." We are getting on but on where?

With some it is a fever of getting or spending, amassing the wealth of earth. The love of money is the root of all evil and men are sick of that root disease. With some it is a fever of worry, fear, doubt, all of them close kin. With some it is ambition. Napoleon had a fever. Today Hitler and Mussolini have it. And we lesser fry do not escape it. With some it is an evil spirit of unlove, bitterness, grudges that fester and create a fever that spoils all peace and joy.

There is no peace to the wicked for they are like the troubled sea when it cannot rest whose waters cast up mire and dirt. Christians too do not enter into God's rest and so live in a fever of self and flesh.

They told Jesus of the woman sick of a fever. "Are you weary? Are you heavy-hearted? Tell it to Jesus" says the old hymn and that is the only recourse that travails. We tell our souls to flee like a bird to this and that mountain but there is rest only in the Lord. Notice that others told Jesus of this case. We are to bring our fevered loved ones to the Lord.

He came and lifted her up and the fever left her. How true through out the ages! His touch turned James and John, sons of thunder, into calm, steady witnesses. His touch transformed Simon Peter; wilful, impulsive, into a rock. His touch transformed Saul, zealous Pharisee, into a mighty preacher. That does not mean that we become lifeless and dull when the fever departs. To put off the old man is not to put on the old woman. When we suffer from a fever, we are of no benefit to others, we are taken up with ourselves. It is when we are freed from the fever that we can help others, being set free from ourselves.

That leads us to the last consideration. The woman arose and ministered unto others. The Lord wants to heal our fevers so that we may serve Him with joy and peace. Serving Christ is the joyful expression of souls set free from their fevers and now free to help others. And there is no fretting in such service.

What is your fever? Let Him heal you that you may minister.

"Lord of the Sabbath"
June 9, 1935

Three of the Gospels (Mt. 12: 1-2; Mk. 2:23-3:12; Lk 5:1-11) record our Lord's Sabbath day experience in the barley fields, His conflict with the Pharisees on that point, and the healing of the withered hand. He and His disciples did not violate the Law in eating the corn for it was expressly permitted in Dt. 23:25, but they simply violated Jewish tradition imposed by scribes and Pharisees. Our Lord gave an unanswerable five-fold argument for His attitude toward the Sabbath. He cited the case of David and the shewbread, the fact that the priests were busy on the Sabbath, the reference to Hosea about God desiring mercy rather than sacrifice, the fact that the Sabbath was made for man rather than man for the Sabbath, and then the climax of all, that He Himself was Lord of the Sabbath. There are those today who overlook the fact that the Sabbath was done away with in Christ along with all Jewish ordinances. We observe the Lord's Day, not because of any definite New Testament command but because it was the day of our Lord's resurrection, the meeting day of the early church and because it meets the principle of one day of rest in seven. We are not to judge one another in regard to days (Col. 2:16) unless false doctrine arises which would revert to legalism instead of the principle of grace. Nor is Sunday a

"Christian Sabbath." The Sabbath was never changed but it was abolished and we are not under law.

After His break with the Pharisees our Lord went into their synagogue, "their" synagogue, mind you, and healed the man with the withered hand. Mark tells us that He looked on His accusers with anger. He had nothing but anger for that religiousness which put a custom above human need. We talk much of the meek and lowly Jesus but there were other aspects to His character. We need to recover His hatred of sin, His condemnation of whatever stood in the way of the will of God and the good of others.

The healing of the withered hand, far from bringing joy to those who witnessed it, only fanned the flames of opposition. What a depravity that can make of such a blessing and incentive to murder! But that is exactly what occurred here for our Lord's enemies took counsel how they might destroy Him. No wonder that it should be the unpardonable sin when men can become so impervious to good as that!

Jesus withdrew to the sea followed by multitudes whom He healed. Matthew here shows the fulfillment of Isaiah 42:1-4 in our Lord, God's chosen servant, in Whom He is well pleased, upon Whom is His Spirit, showing mercy to the Gentiles, not striving nor crying. His voice not heard in the streets. He turned meekly from Israel arrayed against Him because the time for judgment had not come. He would not break the bruised reed nor quench the smoking flax until His second advent. Meanwhile the Gentiles in this present age trust in Him.

"The Unpardonable Sin"
August 11, 1935

Three of the gospels (Mt. 12:22-45; Mk. 3:20-30; Lk. 11:14-36) related the healing of the blind and dumb demoniac, and the controversy that followed. While the people were much impressed the Pharisees accused our Lord of being in league with the devil. His answer was withering: "If I am in league with Satan, then he is fighting himself. Then by what power do your exorcists cast out devils?"

He then speaks of Himself as the: "stronger man" who binds the devil. Either we are with Christ or against Him: "He that is not with me is against me; and he that gathereth not with me scattereth abroad." There is no middle ground. Our Lord also gave the parable of the man who cleaned up his house, made a superficial reformation, but ended more devil-possessed than before. Christ, the stronger man, must take the devil's place in our hearts. The Christian life is not a mere cleaning-up, it is the possessing and filling of the life by Christ Himself. Otherwise it ends worse than it began.

Jesus also declared that since words reveal the heart they will justify or condemn us in the day of judgment. Out of the abundance of the heart the mouth speaketh. He gave them the sign of Jonah signifying His death and resurrection. Remember that all depends upon His being raised from the dead. If He rose not our preaching and faith are vain (1 Cor. 15:14-19.)

But what has concerned readers most in this passage is our Lord's statement about the sin of blasphemy against the Holy Ghost which has no forgiveness. Since words reveal the inner state, the blasphemy of the Pharisees in attributing Christ's work to the devil revealed their inner condition and it is that inner state rather than any act that is beyond forgiveness. The spoken blasphemy is but the expression of the condition of a heart that has become impervious to good, has so long hardened itself against the light and resisted the truth that it regards good as evil. It is possible to reach such a condition in which one is so calloused to the good that it no longer makes any impression. It is not so much that they could not be saved if they wanted to be, or that God refuses to save them, as that they do not want to be saved and manifest not interest whatever.

Unfortunately many people have worried themselves sick thinking they had committed this sin when the very fact that they are concerned shows they are not in such a condition. The very mark of the unpardonable sin is utter indifference to the light and the pleadings of the Spirit. Those who are guilty are not worrying about it.

But here is a warning not to resist too long the Gospel call. Just as every day one goes barefoot the feet become more toughened, so it is with the soul that tramples daily the grace of God.

> "There is a time, I know not when
> A place, I know not where
> Which marks the destiny of men
> To heaven or despair;
> There is a line by us unseen
> Which crosses every path
> The hidden boundary between

"The Unpardonable Sin"

God's patience and His wrath.
How long will men go on in sin?
How long will God forbear?
Where does hope end and where begin
The confines from those skies is sent,
Ye who from God depart,
While it is called today, repent
And harden not your heart."

"The Family of the Spirit"
August 18, 1935

Often we overlook the rich truths contained in those little incidents in the life of our Lord which take up little space and therefore receive too little attention. One such is found in the visit of His relatives (Mt. 12:46-50; Mk. 3:31-35; Lk. 8:19-21.) The brothers of our Lord were puzzled by His ministry. John tells us that they did not believe in Him (7:5.) Far from Mary, His mother, being that faultless character which she has been made to be our Lord made clear to her several times by gentle rebuke His greater loyalty to the Father (Lk. 2:48; John 2:4.)

Now, while He was teaching the people, it appears that His mother and brethren made a rather unseasonable visit, perhaps to caution Him not to overtax Himself or maybe to warn Him not to bring down the wrath of the Pharisees. It is easy to see how well-meaning relatives could interfere with One Who was pursuing a course so certain to bring trouble and so dangerously unusual.

Our Lord's answer, like so many of His replies, was abrupt and seemingly severe but it was meant to bring out a great truth in a way that would command attention and make the audience sit up and take notice. He asks, "Who is my mother? and who are my brethren?" then He declares as

He points out His disciples, "Behold my mother and my brethren! For whosoever shall do the will of my Father which is in heaven the same is my brother and sister and mother." He was declaring that His family was the spiritual fellowship of all who do the will of God. He was not ignoring or despising earthly relationships which have their place and value; He was simply taking opportunity to illustrate the higher relationship of all who are children of God by faith in Himself.

This explains such sharp demands as that we must hate father and mother and wife and children and brethren and sisters and our own lives if we are to be his disciples (Lk. 14:26.) So much greater and higher is this heavenly relationship that our love for our relatives must be as hate compared with our love for Him. It also explains His terse refusal to let would-be disciples return home to bury their dead or bid their families goodbye (Lk. 9:59-62.) No ties of flesh and blood, no relationships of earth, are worthy to hinder our utter abandon to Him. We must ever beware of those, even of our families, who would tone us down or cramp our freedom with even the most well-meant advices if they run counter to His will.

While, of course, this truth can be misapplied to the point of fanaticism, few today have reached its point of loyalty to the highest that will brook no interference from even the closest hearts of earth. Many a man is hampered in his ministry today because of a divided affection. He allows a break in His work for the Father to confer with the relatives who wait.

"What Manner of Man!"
September 15, 1935

Full of truth for us today is the Gospel account of our Lord stilling the tempest (Mt. 8:23-27; Mk. 4:35-41; Lk. 8:22-25). Matthew tells us (8:18) that when Jesus saw great multitudes about Him He gave orders to depart unto the other side of the sea. There is a time to mix with and minister to the crowd and there is also a time to leave the crowd. Some of us in our zeal to serve stay with the crowd when we need to get away for rest and renewed strength.

Mark says the disciples took the Lord "even as He was" in the ship. Tired from the busy day He soon fell asleep. The storm must have been terrific for these disciples were seasoned fishermen for the most part, used to the waves and yet they were alarmed. But no matter how fierce the tempest they had seen our Lord perform His miracles, had witnessed His power over nature, and they should not have given way to panic. How typical of human nature! We believe in a Christ who works wonders. We believe, theoretically, in His supernatural power, but when the actual crisis arises we are terrified. No wonder that He asks, "Why are ye so fearful? How is it that ye have no faith?"

This incident has been misinterpreted again and again. We have heard it applied in this way: Christ asleep in the boat is Christ in the believer, dormant, not called into action, but when the crisis arises we may call upon Him and be delivered. But this is erroneous. If the disciples had more faith they would not have awakened our Lord, they would have let Him sleep. It was fear and not faith that led them to arouse Him. Besides, Christ is not supposed to be a dormant guest in our hearts, to be aroused only in emergency. He abides in us and if we trusted as we ought we would rest in peace in any storm because although at times He may seem to be asleep we are sure of the fact of His presence and that is enough.

We have grown accustomed to hearing this familiar story but if we valued it aright we should cry our as did these disciples: "What manner of man is this, that even the wind and the sea obey Him?" Here He manifested His power over wind and wave for all things are subject to Him by Whom and for Whom all things were made.

Mark also adds the significant little note: "And there were also with Him other little ships." We are not alone upon life's sea, Other lives share in our blessing and if the Lord is with us His benefits to us reach out and indirectly bless others. All the little ships profited from our Lord's presence in one ship. The ship that carries Jesus liveth not unto itself. Even lives in which He does not dwell personally are benefitted by His presence in our lives.

Is the Lord in your boat? At times He may seem asleep, He may answer you not a word, He may tarry as He did in Lazarus' sickness but rest assured that if He be present all things shall work together for good. Do not awaken Him in panic, rest upon His word, "Where is your faith?"

"Only Believe"
September 29, 1935

There is much comfort for us in the healing of the woman with the issue of blood (Mt. 9:18-26; Mk. 5:21-43; Lk. 8:40-56) which is so interwoven with the healing of Jairus' daughter that we give here the scripture including both. This poor woman had the double aggravation of being ill and having spent all on doctors in vain, a circumstance familiar to many of us. Doubtless her faith was rather crude and perhaps mixed with some superstition but it was such faith as she had and she used it. The Word does not stress the quality of it (except to say that a little will work wonders, Mt. 17:29) but the object of faith and since Christ was the object here the blessing followed as it always does.

Our Lord called her back to make it clear that she had been healed through no magical virtue of His but because of her faith. "According to your faith be it unto you," He declared long ago but still we do not believe it, we try roundabout methods to secure what comes only by believing.

This was made clear in this same passage in the case of Jairus. He had summoned Jesus to help his daughter who was at the point of death. While our Lord dealt with the woman some one came from Jairus' house to say, "Thy daughter is dead: why troublest thou the Master any further?" Ah, that is always the attitude of this poor world.

"My case is hopeless, why pray?" But our Lord answered, "Be not afraid, only believe." Would that we could hear Him today in the moment when all seems lost, when fondest hopes have perished, when dearest ones lie dead, saying still as still He does, "Be not afraid, only believe." No matter what your circumstance, keep your confidence in Him and He will do what is for the best. There come so many times when the voice of others, the voice of the evil one says, "What is the use in calling on the Lord? It is a dead prospect, why trouble Him any further?" But there never was a situation in which faith is not the victory. He may not raise our dead as He did then but He will raise them one day and there is no occasion to be afraid for we know that all things work together for good to them who are His.

So He went on into this "impossible" situation and when He declared the maid not dead but only asleep they laughed Him to scorn. Still the world laughs at Him as He moves among our "impossible" situations, our sorrows and broken hopes. "What good does it to trust in Jesus? What can He do for you?" But every day those who trust Him know that He still works His wonders if we only believe.

"One Thing Thou Lackest"
May 24, 1936

There is no more touching scene in all the life of our Lord than His blessing the little children (Mt. 19:13-15; Mk. 10:13-16; Lk. 18:15-17.) Let it never be forgotten that the true Christian is child-like. We often think that the walk of faith is a profound matter that only a few can learn when really it is a simple matter that few ever reach because they will not unlearn down to its simplicity. To be converted and become as little children was our Lord's way of stating it (Mt. 18:3) but that does not appeal to our vanity and pride so very few ever meet those plain terms.

The incident of the rich young ruler (Mt. 19:16-22; Mk. 10:17-22; Lk. 18:18-23) sets forth a model young man who still lacks something and knows it but does not meet the demand of Christ. How Jesus always put His finger on the weak spot in every life! Here the trouble was in the young man's great possessions so that must be removed. He would not be saved by giving up his possessions but his possessions were the hindrance that must be cleared before he could ever be a disciple.

Some do not like negative preaching today and they tell us we should never emphasize giving up but here our Lord certainly did, as in many other cases.

There is irony in the statement that the young man went

away grieved because "he had great possessions." As a matter of fact, he had nothing and had missed his chance of true riches.

Jesus commented on the difficulty of a rich man entering heaven, not because he is rich so much as because he must become as though he had nothing and be poor in spirit, and very few will do that. A rich man need not give up his property unless specially led to do so, but he must be as though he had it not.

Our Lord went on to give the parable of the laborers in the vineyard who went to work at different hours, yet each received the same pay (Mt. 20:1-16.) It can be understood only in the light of what has just gone before. Peter had just spoken of his having forsaken all to follow Jesus as though he expected greater reward for the disciples than for others. But we learn here that God has no favorites, that all receive the same reward in kind if not in degree. The disciples expected greater reward because they followed earlier but Paul and Stephen and Barnabas outshone most of them later. The whole story is based upon the principle, "the first shall be last and the last first." That principle still is true and we cannot measure reward by our own estimates, by length of service or any other external considerations.

Many are called with a general calling but few are chosen because few respond. And there is no favoritism among those chosen. The reward of all servants is to dwell in God's Presence. Men may have varying capacities for the enjoyment of this reward but God Himself is our reward as He told Abraham. Above all else stands the sovereignty of God and His right to manage His own business as He pleases. Jesus does not try to teach everything in one parable and we do wrong to try to cover too much in one lesson. This simply teaches impartiality in God's rewards.

"The Faith of God"
November 23, 1936

Our Lord, in the presence of the withered fig tree, said to His disciples: "Have faith in God." (Mk. 11:22). Really He said, "Have the faith of God." Then He went on to say, "Whosoever shall say unto this mountain, be thou removed, and be thou cast into the sea; and shall not doubt in his heart, but shall believe that those things which he saith shall come to pass; he shall have whatsoever he saith. Therefore I say unto you, what things soever ye desire, when ye pray, believe that ye receive them, and ye shall have them."

Now here is a bona fide promise in black-and-white and if we actually believed these words our lives would be revolutionized until we should almost need to be introduced to ourselves. What kind of faith is this?

It is God's faith, not ours. We cannot stir up mountain-moving faith. It is the same faith by which we believe unto salvation (Eph. 2:8). The faith by which we live is the faith of the Son of God, not merely faith in Him (Gal. 2:20). Yet the sinner must will to believe: when he does, God gives him faith to believe. This same faith he must now exercise and it increases by exercises. And don't forget that it is nourished on the Word of God: "Faith cometh by hearing and hearing by the Word of God" (Rom. 10:17). "Many of them which heard the word believed" (Acts 4:4).

This faith desires: "What things soever ye desire." Only those who hunger and thirst after righteousness really are filled, and only those who really desire great things from God ever get them. There is no real concern today, no burden to see mountains move.

God's faith forgives. Our Lord goes on to say in Mk. 11:25, 26, that we are to forgive and that if we forgive not, our Father will not forgive. We can pray with confidence toward God only when our hearts condemn us not, and an unforgiving spirit does not make for a conscience void of offense.

Then God's faith asks, "Every one that asketh receiveth." We are told to ask, seek, knock, which means progressive praying that moves on with importunity until it gets what it seeks. Here is no superficial sentence-praying but real supplication and intercession.

God's faith wills. Jesus said to the Syrophenician woman, "O woman, great is thy faith: be it unto thee even as thou wilt" (Mt. 15:28). When we are fully yielded to God, He works in us both to will and to do of His good pleasure (Phil. 2:13). He wills through us the things that are in His will and such things of course we receive.

God's faith commands: "Whosoever shall say Be thou removed." God has told us to command Him concerning the work of His hands (Isa. 45:11). When we pray the prayer of faith we may come boldly for we speak with the authority of another.

God's faith believes. 'Having asked and commanded, it believes it shall receive.' Like Hannah, the believer goes away with his countenance no more sad, resting in the Lord. Like Abraham, he staggers not at the promise of God.

God's faith never fails. We are plainly promised that we shall receive. God's faith will remove any mountain God wants moved. A life utterly yielded, fed on the Word, with sin confessed, seeking God's glory–in such a life God will plant a mighty faith that will move mountains.

"Almost to Jesus"
October 10, 1937

The scribe who spoke well the heart of the law, Jesus said, "Thou art not far from the kingdom of God" (Mk. 12:34). But one may almost reach salvation and still be lost. A soldier, after going through the war in France, was killed in a wreck when he had almost reached his home in America. Almost, but lost!

Some get as far as the church. The father brought his demonized boy to the disciples but they could not heal him. Then Jesus came and said, "Bring him to me" (Mt. 17:14-21). Today a powerless church stands before needy souls and all too often it must be said of us disciples, "And thy could not". We can do no mighty works because of unbelief. And men lambast the church and talk of the mistakes and failures of the church. But back of the church stands the Lord saying, "Bring him to me. I have not failed. The church cannot save. You must get through to me." To be sure this does not excuse the weakness of the church. Such power comes only by prayer and fasting and the church will not fast and pray today. But men need to know that it is not enough to get as far as the church and into the church. Press through to Jesus!

Some get as far as the Bible. "Ye search the Scriptures: for in them ye think ye have eternal life and they are they which testify of me. And ye will not come to me that ye might have life" (John 5:39, 40). One may study the Bible in an academic way and never know its Christ. This scribe we started with knew his Scripture but not the Lord. To be an expert in a biography is not to know the subject of the biography. And greater is the condemnation if we know the Bible and know not Christ. The heathen has not that condemnation. To read travel folders is not to travel. All roads in the book lead to Christ: but do you travel the road?

Some get as far as doctrine. At the grave of Lazarus, Jesus said to Martha, "Thy brother shall rise again". She said, "I know that he shall rise again in the resurrection at the last day". Martha was orthodox, she was correct in her doctrine, a good fundamentalist. But our Lord changed the emphasis from the doctrinal to the person: "I am the resurrection and the life, he that believeth in me, though he were dead, yet shall he life: And whosoever liveth and believeth in me shall never die. Believest thou this?" He made the resurrection not something to believe but someone to believe and it brought personal confession from Martha;" "I believe that Thou art the Christ, the Son of God, which should come into the world". One may know doctrine and not know Him. It is not he that believes in the resurrection but he who believes in Him Who rose who is saved.

Certainly one who comes to Him will belong to the church, read the Bible and believe doctrine. But back of all these stands Christ Himself. The devil will have men join the church and become theologically orthodox if only they do not touch Christ. And one may come almost to Christ. Jostle Him in the crowd but never touch Him and feel His virtue.

Be sure you get through to Jesus!

"The Divine Paradox"
July 2, 1933

While Jesus hung upon the cross the chief priests mocking said among themselves, with the scribes, "He saved others; Himself He cannot save" (Mk. 15:31).

In their scorn they were declaring a truth greater than they knew. While they meant to belittle Him the real truth of their statement is to His eternal glory. To save others He must give Himself: it is the stupendous heart of the atonement. "Without shedding of blood is no remission" (Heb. 9:22).

In a lesser sense, and one applicable to you and me, it was also a fulfilment of Jesus' own paradox, "Whosoever will save his life shall lose it; but whosoever will lose his life for my sake, the same shall save it" (Lk. 9:24). If Jesus had decided, in Gethsemane, to save His life He would have lost it as our Saviour: but in losing it He truly saved it as our Redeemer.

Here is the application for us: In saving others we cannot save ourselves. I speak of saving others in the sense of winning them to Christ and God. If we are to rescue others we must expect to spend and be spent. So long as life revolves around self, self-advancement, self-promotion, self-satisfaction, we are wretched and miserable. If we are to save others we must forget ourselves. When the family is sick, mother forgets herself in caring for others and generally the Lord seems to keep mothers going in such times. In service we Christians must lose ourselves with the spirit of Paul: "Neither count I my life dear unto myself" (Acts 20:24).

Then there is the other side of the paradox: In losing our lives to save others we most truly save ourselves. I am not here speaking of saving our souls, no good works can save the soul, but faith in Christ only. We can save our lives, our time, our talents as we spend them in saving others. The only time you ever save is the time you spend for others. The only money you ever save is the money you spend for others. It is the only certain investment in this gold-brick age. Paul has it in mind when He bids the Ephesians redeem the time. Jesus has it in mind when He says lay up treasure in heaven. It is the principle of the parable of the unjust steward: use your earthly assets to make for yourself friends through service. Bread cast on the waters of service return even if after many days.

How slow men are to learn that in saving life they lose it, in losing it for Christ's sake they save it. Mind you, Jesus said, "Whosoever will lose his life for my sake." Not for one's own sake, not to be called a hero, not for conscience's sake, but for Christ's sake. More idealistic service is not meant here. Often that is a price men offer for salvation.

This is a day of introverted living. We look at everything in the light of self, what it will profit us, where we can gain by this and that move. Christ turns life outward so that selfish Saul, proud of his legal righteousness, becomes a Paul who could wish himself accursed for his brethren's sake. Spend life and you save it; give it and you get it.

We do not save our lives while we save others but because we save others. We often lose our money, our health, our temporal fortunes. But if we leave all for His sake we shall be compensated in this world and in the world to come receive eternal life.

"The Divine Paradox"

In saving others you cannot spare yourself. Yet in saving others you do most surely preserve yourself. All that you save is what you spend on others for His sake.

"Out to See Jesus"
May 31, 1936

There came the day when Jesus told His disciples of His approaching death (Mk. 20:17-19; Mk. 10:32-34; Lk. 18:31-34). He knew from the beginning that He must die. It was no mere happening but part of the Divine plan from all eternity. But beyond the cross He saw also the resurrection.

How distressing is the contrast when immediately after this statement and the parable of laborers, should come the request of James and John for favored places in His kingdom! How much they had to learn! They were to drink of the cup of persecution but only God could award places. Jesus rebuked the spirit that seeks the upper places. We are great only as we serve. He Himself declares that He came to give His life a ransom for many–a clear statement of the atonement.

Bartimaeus is a type of the sinner, blind and begging. No matter what else you see or what else you own, if Christ has not opened your eyes, you are a blind beggar. Bartimaeus cried out. Emotion has been outlawed in our churches but if sinners truly realized their plight they would cry for mercy while Jesus is passing by. Notice that some tried to discourage Bartimaeus and even Christians may discourage earnest seekers but Jesus can hear the sinners cry over all the din and tumult. Notice that Bartimaeus knew what he needed first and most, his sight. And when he received it he followed Christ, glorifying God. That is the Christian experience, first the new sight, then following the Lord with joy.

Zacchaeus was a tax-collector for Rome and a Jew which made a despised combination. But he sought to see Jesus. We crowd the streets when the President passes but how many go to pains to see Jesus. Zacchaeus was little of stature and could not get through the crowd. The things that get in ones way when he starts out to see Jesus! These people also were out to see Jesus so sometime even good people with good intentions get in the way of the seeking sinner. But Zacchaeus would not be discouraged, he climbed a sycamore. There is always a sycamore for the man who really wants a blessing. Of course it was not dignified to climb the tree but when a man really wants to get through to Jesus he will forget dignity and custom and press through the crowd or tear up the roof or climb a tree to get through to Christ. How we need a holy desperation today that will not be stopped short of Jesus!

Mind you, Zacchaeus was on the right road, "for He was to pass that way." There are some roads Christ does not travel, pride, haughtiness, mere morality, skepticism. And Jesus saw Zacchaeus. Christ is always looking for the seeking soul. He told Zacchaeus He was going home with him. Christ wants to live with us, not merely meet us at church. And Zacchaeus came down in haste and received Him joyfully and offered to make restitution for all his past money-grabbing. It is a fine evidence of regeneration when a man takes back things that don't belong to him. This man's faith hit his pocketbook! He was not saved because he did this, he did this because he was saved. He was a double child of Abraham, by flesh and by faith.

Jesus is passing by. Set out to see Him though you must climb a sycamore.

PART THREE

REFLECTIONS ON THE GOSPEL OF LUKE

"Thy Prayer is Heard"
January 20, 1935

Zacharias had prayed through long, lean years for a son. He and Elizabeth had many qualifications for a life of blessing–good ancestry, they "were righteous before the Lord," not merely before men, they walked in all the commandments of the Lord blameless, not faultless but living up to their light.

But there follows the sad statement: "And they had no child." Have you sought to live the blameless life, yet your piety seems to have borne no progeny, you are barren? Remember Zacharias. It was now too late, from the natural viewpoint, to have a son but Zacharias had not forgotten his altar and his duty. He kept offering incense, symbol of thanksgiving, when there seemed so little to be thankful for. Do not forsake your incense and the angel will yet appear!

The herald from heaven announces a son. God often waits until it is too late with us; it is never too late with Him. Poor Zacharias is doubtful. And doubt leads to dumbness–it always does. When we do not trust we have no testimony. But God fails not, though Zacharias does. The baby is born and when neighbors would name him for his father, Zacharias puts God first and names Him by the Divine direction. Do not name things after yourself, give God the glory. Then dumbness gives way to delight: Zacharias speaks and so will you!

John was to drink neither wine nor strong drink but was to be filled with the Spirit. Three times the New Testament sets wine and the Spirit in contrast (Lk. 1:15; Acts 2:13; Eph. 5:18.) Wine changes face, walk, talk, stimulates, so does the Spirit.

God was fulfilling here the prophecy made in Mal. 4:5, 6. How marvelously His plans work out exactly on schedule; Zacharias, filled with the Holy Ghost, breaks into prophecy of a Jewish cast setting forth the glory of the coming Christ. God has visited His people to redeem them. We must bear in mind here that Christ came first to Israel. Zacharias knows He is to be of the house of David, a testimony to His royal lineage. Prophecy is fulfilled, promises performed, the holy covenant remembered. Notice how complete is this redemption: Freedom, "being delivered out of the hand of our enemies;" Purpose, "that we might serve Him;" Nature of this service, "without fear in holiness and righteousness before Him;" the duration, "all the days of our life."

Then Zacharias turns to his own son who is to be called the prophet of the Highest to go before the face of the Lord to prepare Him ways, to give knowledge of salvation, light to them that sit in darkness and the shadow of death, to guide our feet into the way of peace. This salvation is through God's tender mercy whereby the "dayspring from on high," probably the Branch of Isa. 11:1 and Zech. 3:8 hath visited us.

John grows and waxes strong in the spirit in the desert solitude till the day of his appearing to Israel. There is some difference between this and the closing verse of the next chapter where Jesus, living a more social life, increases also in favor with man.

"Blessed Among Women"
January 27, 1935

The beautiful story of the annunciation of the birth of Christ to Mary has suffered from over-emphasis among some and under-emphasis among others. Mary has been called "The Mother of God" which she was not. She was the mother of the Man Christ Jesus. She was "highly favored" and "blessed among women" for exactly this reason because God had chose her to be the Virgin mother of His only begotten Son as pertaining to the flesh. There is a Mariolatry which ignores our Lord's own attitude toward His mother.

Gen. 3:15 now received fulfilment and "the seed of the woman" is coming to bruise the serpent's head. Isaiah 7:14 here comes to fulfillment in the Son Immanuel. He is to reign over the house of Jacob from the throne of David, a prophecy yet to be fulfilled; Christ is at the right hand of the throne of God but not now on the Throne of David.

It is significant that the first question asked about the virgin birth was asked by the virgin herself. "How shall this be?" Men have asked it ever since but here is God's own answer that it is the supernatural work of the Holy Ghost and the power of God. Much argument is focused on the supernatural birth instead of the supernatural Son. The Son of God required a birth in keeping with His deity. Who He is explains how He was born.

Mary goes to Elizabeth with the good news and breaks forth into the Magnificat (Lk. 1:46-55. Very similar is Hannah's prophetic prayer in 1 Sam. 2:1-10, both closing with reference to Christ, "His king" with Hannah and the "Help" promised Israel with Mary. The theme through both is the marvelous way in which God puts down the mighty and exalts those of low degree even as He still does in His choosing of the saints (1 Cor. 1:26-31.)

Elizabeth, filled with the Holy Ghost, had already called Mary "the mother of my Lord." So she was but mother of Him a man and in no way that elevates her to be worthy of worship. Bengel rightly says she is addressed as a daughter of grace, not as the mother of it (Lk. 1:28.)

A beautiful little lesson in faith is gathered from verses 34, 37, and 45. "How shall this be?"–that is the query of men since the beginning when faced with the message of the supernatural power of God. The natural man cannot receive nor comprehend how God works His wonders of grace.

The answer is "With God nothing shall be impossible" (v. 37). God is able to save (Heb. 7:25), to keep (Jude 24), to succor (Heb. 2:18), to deliver (Dan. 3:17), to do (Eph. 3:20), to subdue (Phi. 3:21).

Then verse 45: "And blessed is she that believed: for there shall be a performance of those things which were told her of the Lord." It is always so when we take Him at His word. He who promises will perform. Do not ask "How?" Take Him at His Word and it shall be done even as He has said.

"No Room For Jesus"
December 25, 1938

As this Christmas day brings us around once more to the blessed story of the Savior's birth, it reminds us of a circumstance connected with that event which still is timely in its application. When Joseph and Mary came to Bethlehem they were forced to put up in a stable "because there was no room for them in the inn." (Lk. 2:7).

Today, amid this commercialized Christmas, this overworked headache of expensive giving, God's great gift, the first Christmas gift, stands often unrecognized. It is easy enough to sing Christmas carols and put on pageants, the tribute of our lips, but how many of us honestly face Christ Himself and His challenge of discipleship at any cost? There is room for many things today, room even for much about Jesus but is there room for Him?

Let it be observed, so far as we know, this inn-keeper may not have been unkind or discourteous to Joseph and Mary. I don't read that he drove them away when they came to him. He may have been very polite and even expressed his regrets but, just the same, there was no room for them. So today most people turn down the Lord because they are preoccupied. They have nothing against Him, they may even speak well of Him but there is no room, their hearts and homes are filled with other things. So today, men have bought land and oxen and married wives and cannot entertain the Lord Jesus, their time and thought are already taken up with other things, maybe not bad things but things too important for what they are worth.

This inn-keeper may have said, "Come back tomorrow, some other day." So men say that at some more convenient season they will accept the Lord. They do not really mean to pass Him up, the house is just too full now and after they have straightened up things a bit and made more room, then He will be welcomed. But days lengthen into weeks and months and years and life has gone and there has never been room enough for Jesus.

What other guests do you have in your heart and home that shut out Jesus? For certainly the reason why there is no room is because there are others in His place. Is there anybody or anything in all this universe important enough to take His place? Eternity lies ahead and you had better admit the guest Who can spend it with you. You will need Him out there. Remember the man who cleaned out his house but left it empty and seven devils returned. It is not even enough to clear out undesirable guests. If Jesus does not take the place of what goest out, the latter state will be worse than the first. God cannot use an empty heart, a vacant life will soon be devil-filled.

I beg of you, on this Christmas day, do not make of it a hollow mockery by paying a wordy tribute to the Christ while you refuse Him your heart. It does no good to go to church and listen to cantatas if you have barred and bolted your heart against the Christ. Today He would enter as Saviour and Lord. One day He will come as Judge and then you cannot escape Him.

Be sure to put the Christ in Christmas!

"Tempted Like As We"
March 3, 1935

The three-fold temptation of our Lord corresponds to the temptation of the first Adam in Genesis. John tells us (1 Jn. 2:16) that the threefold appeal is by the lust of the flesh, the lust of the eye, and the pride of life. This appeal was used with Eve; "when the woman saw that the tree was good for food, and that it was a delight to the eyes, and that the tree was to be desired to make one wise, she took the fruit thereof, and did eat; and she gave also unto her husband with her, and he did eat." (Gen. 3:6)

Luke in his account of the Son of Man follows the Genesis order but Matthew puts the third appeal second making the order that which would appeal most to the King with its offers of a quick way to the throne.

Jesus meets the appeal to the flesh with the Sword of the Spirit, the Word of God. He could have provided Himself a meal for God can set a table in the wilderness whenever He likes, but our Lord was willing to trust God to supply His need without resorting to the suggestion of the devil. He will not selfishly use His power.

Then the devil undertook to pervert the Word of God and lead Jesus to resort to the spectacular to prove God's care. He quotes a Messianic Psalm in which God promises to protect the Messiah because He is obedient and trustful.

Had He listened to satan He would have broken the condition. To ever ask signs and wonders of God, to demand some sensational proof of His love and care is to follow this same suggestion of the devil.

Then the adversary offered the Lord the kingdoms of this world. They really were his to offer for this present world-system is under him. In John 12:31 and 14:30 our Lord speaks of satan as the "prince of this world" and in 2 Cor. 4:4 calls him the "god of this world." God owns the world but the devil possesses it in the present age. But Jesus defeated the tempter again with a sword-thrust from Deuteronomy. No wonder the devil has fought Deuteronomy so and has sought to destroy it with higher criticism! The Lord defeated him each time with a verse from that book. If the Lord used only three verses from Deuteronomy to whip the devil we ought to put up a good fight with the whole Bible!

Mark adds that our Lord was with the wild beasts. The first Adam was tempted in a lovely garden with all creation at peace. The second Adam was tempted in a wilderness typical of the earth spoiled by sin. But one day, by reason of His victory, He shall reign over the earth redeemed from the curse and with creation at peace (Isa. 11:6-8; Rom. 8:18-25.)

After the devil left Him angels ministered to Jesus. After each victory over evil we are visited by His strengthening Presence in fresh power, in joy and in confidence. Luke adds significantly that the devil departed "for a season." Through His life our Lord suffered being tempted and is able to succor them that are tempted (Heb. 2:18.)

"Lepers are Cleansed, the Lame Walk"
May 19, 1935

Matthew, Mark and Luke record the healing of a leper who came to our Lord saying, "If Thou wilt, Thou canst make me clean." With him the question was not of Christ's power but of His willingness. The Saviour touched him–ceremonial defilement, mind you, for this man was a loathsome leper–and healed him. Our Lord is willing to touch and transform the vilest. The leper was bidden not to publish the healing of Jesus did not want to stir up sensationalism and He knew the superficiality of public enthusiasm. He bade the leper fulfil the Levitical legal requirement, a good reminder for those who foolishly disregard all tradition and precedent. The leper, contrary to instructions, broadcasted what had happened to him and one finds it hard to blame him! Luke adds the significant detail about our Lord, "And He withdrew Himself into the wilderness and prayed." Gathering multitudes and growing popularity, far from lessening His hours of prayer, increased them and drove Him all the oftener to the secret place.

Following this miracle our Lord went into Capernaum and taught crowds that jammed the house and we read that "the power of the Lord was present to heal them" (Lk. 5:17). Four friends of a paralytic carried the sick man to be healed and were forced to tear up the roof and let him down into the presence of Jesus. Certainly this was undignified and unconventional procedure but any course is justifiable that brings a man to the Lord. There would be more miracles today if there were more roofs torn up, more believers willing to do the unusual thing to get the needy to the lord.

The record says "When Jesus saw their faith." Our faith and prayer and efforts bring blessing to others. Jesus began by forgiving the man's sins. This was boldest claim to be the Son of God and it astounded the scribes and Pharisees who reasoned that only God could forgive sins. Their reasoning was entirely correct on that score but what they did not see was that God was before them in the person of His Son.

Our Lord then gave a visible evidence that he had power to do the invisible wonder of forgiving sins. They could not tell whether the man had been forgiven or not but when he arose and walked they could all see that he had been healed! He had come in with his back on his bed and he went out with his bed on his back and there was no denying that!

We read that the people glorified God saying.."We never saw it on this fashion." Indeed not! How this sad old world needs today to witness the wonder of a miracle-working Christ! But He cannot do many mighty works because of our unbelief. If we had faith to carry the needy to Him, persistence enough to tear up any roof that bars the way, He would reward our faith with wondrous blessing. Alas, we have dropped to a pale and pitiful dignity that respectfully gathers at church–and most of us don't even do that–but there is not that determined, vivid, roof-raising faith that will not be denied. Let us return to that and men will say once more, "We never saw it of this fashion."

"As Thou Hast Believed"
July 7, 1935

Our Lord, having healed elsewhere, returns to Capernaum and brings blessing at home as well as abroad (Mt. 8:5-13; Lk. 7:1-10). A Roman centurion comes to Him in behalf of a sick servant. How we ought always to come to our Lord in behalf of others and not only of the high and mighty but even of servants, the despised and lowly! This centurion had lived up to the light he had, had befriended the Jews and built them a synagogue. Such men always find more light.

His humility is shown in that he though himself unworthy to have the Lord under his roof. That spirit also always gets a blessing. He recognizes that just as he has men under his authority so the Lord has authority over disease. Alas, we today do not believe He can and will work wonders, we see no authority beyond the purely natural. There is little recognition of the sovereignty of our Christ over every problem.

In the simple faith of this centurion our Lord saw a prophetic type of Gentiles being saved while the unbelieving Jews would be cast out (Mt. 8:10-12). How true that is in this present church-age is evident to us all.

Jesus commanded the centurion, "Go thy way; and as those hast believe, so be it done unto thee." It reminds us of His statement to the blind men: "According to your faith be it unto you," (Mt. 9:29). Our faith is the measure of our blessing. As we believe, we receive. How naturally follows the conclusion here: "And his servant was healed in the selfsame hour." We blame many things for our meager, pale and tasteless lives today but we simply do not believe His word enough to go our way. We must see before believing whereas these believed and then went forth to see the wonder wrought.

Next day our Lord entered Nain and met a widow's son being carried to burial. A procession of life met a procession of death. Much people, we read in the account (Lk. 7:11-17) were in each procession. It is not recorded that the widow solicited aid but the Lord saw her and had compassion. With the simple word "Arise" He raised the dead. Three raisings are recorded in the Gospels. One had just died, the daughter of Jairus; this young man was on the way to burial; and Lazarus had been dead four days. But the Lord raised all three and although the details differed each could say, "Once I was dead but now I live." Is it not so in conversion? Elijah and Elisha had raised the dead with great wrestlings but here our Lord simply calls the dead to life.

Of course, after such an event, the people would be in fear and glorify God but most of the response, doubtless, was of that superficial sort that will not believe except it see signs and wonders. Often we think that if Jesus were among us today working such miracles men would believe but not so. Skeptics would offer their explanations, the magicians would produce their counterfeits and sinful men would go on their way loving darkness rather than light. More blessed are they who see not yet believe and, believing, rejoice with joy unspeakable and full of glory.

"The Raising of Lazarus"
May 3, 1936

In Luke 7:1-10 our Lord gives us certain precious truths along several different lines; capsules of consecrated teaching. He declares that offences must come but woe to him by whom they come! Better that a millstone be hanged about his neck and he be cast into the sea. Here we have Divine sovereignty and human free will. The fact that offences must come does not absolve us from blame if we cause offense.

Next, Jesus declared that forgiveness must be unlimited and oft repeated without weariness. It often may be overlooked that He said, "If thy brother trespass against thee, rebuke him" first of all, then, "if he repent, forgive him." We may tell our brother wherein he has offended us and thereby ground may be reached for an understanding. That is better than to hide our resentment in the heart.

The apostles, who doubt seeing that this teaching on forgiveness called for more faith than they had, said, "Lord, increase our faith." I want you to notice Jesus' reply. He did not say He would increase their faith. What He did say was almost a reproof: "If you had faith as a grain of mustard seed, ye might say unto this sycamore tree, Be thou plucked up by the root and be thou planted in the seed and it should obey you." In other words: "It is not the quantity of faith that matters most. If you had even a little, you could be working wonders." We want more faith when even the exercises of a little will do the impossible.

Then our Lord moved onto point out a lesson on duty. He illustrates it by the reference to servants who have worked all day and have done their duty, yet are asked to perform extra tasks outside their regular schedule. It is the principle of the second mile all over again. The first mile is obligation, the second is privilege. Some of us pride ourselves upon doing our duty but here the Lord gives us this startling word: "We are unprofitable servants: we have done that which was our duty to do." Had it ever occurred to you that you could do your duty and still be an unprofitable servant? How many pride themselves on duty and still are only Pharisees, servants but knowing nothing of that "exceeding righteousness" which is Christ Himself.

It is that extra mile of doing things we don't have to do that reveals the Christian spirit. How may are one-mile Christians at prayer, at Bible reading, in their giving, in church-going, in forgiving others? How many in trouble only bear and endure it and go not the second mile of victory? How many in temptation merely suppress and do not surpass? How but will not go the way of consecration and separation? Some will give money but will not give self. We have unduly gloried duty and have failed to see that only Christ within us is true righteousness, that all else is but legalism though it may profess His Name.

"The Blessing of the Unoffended"
July 21, 1935

John the Baptist, rugged, outdoor ascetic, found prison life depressing and sent to know whether Jesus really was the Messiah. Great men may know moods of doubt and despondency. Our Lord simply declared that His works proved His mission, then paid John fine tribute. Here, He declared, was no comfortable, fashionable court preacher but a real prophet, than whom no greater man had arisen. Yet the humblest believer in the age of grace is greater, in point of privilege, than John who lived under law. The difference is in position, not a matter of moral worth.

Our Lord declared that the kingdom suffered violence and the violent took it by force, comparing those who were pressing into the kingdom to soldiers storming a fortress. Verily, the things of God are not for loafers: we must be violently resolute if we are to press into the deeper things; we must be diligent to make calling and election sure. Then He said John was the Elias prophesied in Mal. 4:5,6. Meanwhile, the Pharisees were like spoiled children who could not be suited with any kind of preaching, the fasting of John or the feasting of Jesus. But wisdom is vindicated of her children, in the lives of her disciples, in that wise children receive truth in any garb, and in the sense that wisdom is proven by what she does, the results she produces.

A neglected verse in this account (Mt. 11:1-9; Lk. 7:18-35) is verse six in Matthew and verse 23 in Luke: "And blessed is he whosoever shall not be offended in me." John the Baptist had become offended in the Lord. Jesus was not doing things the way John had expected. He had prophesied a Messiah of flame and fire and Jesus was merely going about doing good. How wide are the applications of this truth!

Believers often are tempted to pout with the Lord like those of Malachi's day who said: "It is vain to serve God; and what profit is it that we have kept His ordinance and that we have walked mournfully before the Lord of hosts?" So men pray and do not receive and, like Martha, when our Lord delayed His coming, they grow rebellious. Others are offended at hard doctrine like those in John 6, or because of persecution as in Mt. 13:21.

Mistaught Christians are grieved today because Christianity is not conquering the world and things are growing worse. But our Lord said it would be so. He is working His wonders still as He did in John's day and is carrying out His plans just as He intended. We have misunderstood His method and mission and message. He will come one day as conquering King but now the blind see, the deaf hear, the lame walk, the lepers are cleansed and the poor have the gospel preached to them. He would have us not to be offended (John 16:1) and if we love His law we shall not be offended (Ps. 119:165.) Our Lord is carrying out His program on schedule time. Let us learn the beatitude of the unoffended.

"For She Loved Much"
August 4, 1935

Luke alone (7:36-50) records the anointing of our Lord in the house of a Pharisee. This man had invited Jesus perhaps out of curiosity or admiration and our Lord who received sinners and ate with them, being a friend of publicans and sinners, accepted the invitation. As He ate, a woman who had been a sinner, doubtless a harlot, in the city, came to Him and anointed His feet. She had likely heard Him teach and came in a state of genuine contrition, godly sorrow and repentance. Such a state manifest itself in brokenness. There is much shallow repentance today because men have such a shallow sense of sin.

The Pharisee reasoned within himself that if Jesus were a prophet He would not have allowed such a contact and defilement. But our Lord, reading his thoughts, gave him the parable of the two debtors, one owing five hundred pence and the other fifty. Both were forgiven: now which loved his creditor most? The plain application as He Himself gave it was that those who are forgiven most love most and this woman, being a grievous sinner and realizing it, was full of gratitude because much was forgiven. While all are sinners and it is not the amount of sins committed that condemns the sinner, yet those who have offended most grievously in degree, though all offend in kind, usually are most grateful.

That explains why men converted from terrible careers of vicious sin often are most exuberant in their testimony and why those saved early and not conscious of years of vile transgression do not generally manifest the same sense of deliverance.

"Her sins, which are many, are forgiven; for she loved much: but to whom little is forgiven, the same loveth little" is not to be taken to mean that the woman was forgiven because she loved. She loved much because she was forgiven much. Her love was the expression of gratitude for sins already forgiven. Some think she had already been forgiven before this incident; others, that Jesus, perceiving in her genuine repentance forgave her at the outset and announced it at the close of the incident.

Our smug and pale Christianity today shows little of that broken and humble gratitude for sins forgiven that marked this woman. Few alabaster boxes are broken in tearful joy over forgiveness. Sin has been glossed over; men do not regard themselves sinners and consequently feel no burden of guilt and, of course, no relief in His pardon. We bring Him verbal tribute, wordy compliments on Sunday but few kneel weeping at His feet.

"Thy faith hath saved thee: go in peace." It is faith that saves so far as our part goes. Of course, Christ the object of our faith, saves us but faith looks unto Him and appropriates His pardon. And because we are forgiven and saved we may go in peace, peace with God through our Lord Jesus Christ, and the peace of God that passeth all understanding.

"Three Gospel Snapshots"
October 11, 1936

In the ninth chapter of his Gospel Luke groups three snapshot incidents from our Lord's ministry so briefly that we are in danger of passing too quickly over the treasure of truth hidden there. Three characters flash suddenly by; we never hear of them again; the tantalizing brevity of it all leaves us wondering what became of them.

The first of these, much impressed by the Master, in a fit of momentary enthusiasm declares: "I will follow you everywhere you go!" Now, Matthew tells us that this man was a scribe and the offer of a recognized rabbi to become a disciple must have looked very attractive. Up until then, only rough fisherman and common workaday folk had volunteered; no influential persona had lined up with Jesus. Now the prominent are professing! You or I might have seized that proposition before he had finished speaking!

But Jesus did not so hastily accept this distinguished convert. Instead He calmly replied: "The foxes have holes and the birds of the air have nests; but the Son of man hath not where to lay His head." A figurative way of saying: "Before you so lightly rush into this adventure of following me, I want you to count the cost. Do you realize what it means: To surrender your home comforts, position, reputation, all prospects of advancement as a rabbi to be the despised disciple of a hated 'fanatic'?"

There it ends. But in a flash it portrays a type all too common: The easily-excited, emotional enthusiast, quick-on-the-trigger, a rapid beginner but the sort that stalls on the middle mile when reality reveals the actual dimensions and cost of the thing he has undertaken. Verily, the Christian adventure is no romantic excursion for the glib and gushing school.

This man was too eager; the next two are not eager enough. The first of these meets Jesus' invitation to follow Him with a condition: "First, let me go bury my father." Whenever a man starts off with "ifs" and "buts" and reservations and provisos, there is something wrong; he has not made a full surrender. Their name is Legion who want to follow Christ but who have not fully turned loose of something dead which they want to bury. Somewhere in their lives there is a corpse, a carcass of money or lust or cherished evil or even something not bad in itself as this man's dead father was not wrong in itself but which is a millstone that holds them back from crossing the line of absolute dedication. They want to go back, they think, to bury it and eventually to fall in love with it all over again and never become a disciple.

So Jesus rings out His "let the dead bury the dead." It sounds harsh but it is the Divine condition. "Give up utterly these dead loves of the old life! I will have no divided allegiance! I must be Lord of all or not at all! If you mean to follow me, I will have no fondling of these carcasses of earth!" And many a soul never has joined the procession of the redeemed because still he lingers among the graves of this world's decaying treasures!

The third man merely wishes to tell his family goodbye; surely there is no harm in that! Yet back comes the stern rejoinder: "No man, having put his hand to the plow, and looking back, is fit for the kingdom of God." The danger

"Three Gospel Snapshots"

was this: if the man went home to say farewell, the chances are he might have stayed. The relatives and neighbors would have cooled his ardor in their commonplace circle–any man who has tried to serve tho King in a matter-of-fact environment knows that full well. "Don't get worked up over this new preacher. You had better reconsider and stay sensibly fixed like you are. This is a fit of fancy and will soon blow over. You know what happened to so-and-so" –thus they would have talked and toned his fiery idealism to a tepid dullness, the drab luke-warmness of those average souls who never see the Heavenly Vision.

So, with this plowman figure, Jesus said in substance: "If you are going with me, let us go. But my road is not for those vacillating mortals with their feet turned one way and their head another, who never know what they want, who never radically break the ties of the world behind them but ever look back, like Lot's wife upon Sodom. My kingdom is no place for the man with the backward look!"

Three marvelous snapshots: The Peril of the Uncounted Cost, the Danger of the Unburied Corpse; the Tragedy of the Unforsaken Circle.

"Three Gospel Snapshots"
February 9, 1936

In Luke 9:51-62 we find our Lord steadfastly setting His face toward Jerusalem, the cross and the consummation of His ministry. The Samaritans refused to receive Him because He headed for Jerusalem. It was quite a different attitude from that of the Samaritans in John 4. The disciples James and John wanted to call down fire from heaven upon them as Elijah had done in 2 Kings 1:10-12. Swift was the reply of our Lord: "Ye know not what manner of spirit ye are of. For the Son of Man is not come to destroy men's lives but to save them."

Christians today would do well to ponder these words. Often we have shown a disposition to call down fire upon others, not knowing what manner of spirit we are of. "Vengeance is mine, I will repay, saith the Lord."

The rest of this passage sets forth three Gospel snapshots. Three men appear suddenly upon the stage and as suddenly they are gone. The tantalizing brevity of it all leaves us wondering what became of them. They illustrate three perils of Christian discipleship, the peril of the uncounted cost, the peril of the unburied corpse and the peril of the unforsaken circle.

The first man, a scribe according to Matthew, was a quick-on-the-trigger enthusiast who simply had not counted the cost. In Luke 14:25-33 our Lord deals thoroughly with this matter in the parables of the tower and the king going to battle. He would have us know what we are doing and count the cost of obedience and following Him.

The second man was invited to discipleship by the Lord Himself but he wanted first to go home and bury his father. The real trouble was in that word "first." Something else came before following the Lord. He was ready to follow but not just yet. Our Lord sternly replied, "Let the dead bury their dead; but go thou and preach the kingdom of God." It is better that the dead should be unburied than that we fail to follow Him. Let the unbelieving relatives bury their dead. Let the dead in trespasses and in sins bury their kind. Whatever interpretation we put upon these words, we gather that our Lord will have no fondling of the carcasses of earth. No obligation of earth, no ties of the sentiment are worthy to hinder our discipleship to Him. Too many Christians sing hymns on Sunday but all week they are out in the world helping the dead to bury their dead.

The third man went further than the second. "I will follow Thee," he said but "first" he would tell his people goodby. "I will follow Thee but–," there is the weakness of many a prospective disciple. Our Lord uses a familiar figure from farm life to declare the peril of looking back. His kingdom is no place for a man with his feet pointed one way and his head the other. We are to forget the things behind. There is no place in discipleship for divided allegiance.

"Fix your eyes upon Jesus" and run the race looking unto Him. Count the cost, let the dead bury the corpse and forsake the circle of those who are at home in this world.

"The 70 and the Samaritan"
February 16, 1936

Our Lord sends out seventy disciples (Lk. 10: 1-24) with a charge similar to that given to the twelve in Matthew 9. Once in a while some literal-minded questioner wants to know why preachers do not now go out without purse or scrip according to these directions. This was local ministry to Israel under conditions vastly different from ours. Later, when His disciples must face a Gentile world, our Lord gave quite different instructions (Lk. 22:35, 36).

Later, the seventy returned with joy reporting that even the devils were subject unto them. Our Lord answers, "I saw Satan as lightning fall from heaven." He was with them in their ministry and saw Satan defeated and here He also sums up in a flash his final defeat even as he fell from heaven (Isa. 14:12-19) long before, a sight which our Lord doubtless beheld. Rev. 12:7-12 also pictures this fall of Satan. Our Lord is assuring them that as He saw Satan fall at first so He sees him finally defeated which is typified by their success in casting out demons.

After giving them power over the enemy our Lord bids them rejoice not in that but that their names are written in heaven. The sole ground of our rejoicing is not in our powers or successes but in the unmerited and undeserved grace of God.

Jesus thanks the Father that the profound truths of heaven have been kept from the wise and prudent and revealed unto babes, the childlike (Mt. 18:3.) He tells His disciples that they are privileged to see what prophets and kings had longed for. Marvelous truth that the greatest revelation of all time was made to the humblest, the simple and lowly disciples who received Him gladly! It has always been so, through the ages in His subsequent revelations through the Spirit. "More blessed are they that see not, yet believe" and "not many wiser mighty and noble are called" (1 Cor. 1:26-31).

The familiar story of the Good Samaritan (Lk. 10:25-37) was given instead of argument of the lawyer who asked, "Who is my neighbor?" He thought only Jews were his neighbors and our Lord makes two Jews pass by in this story while the hero was a Samaritan. This must have been distasteful to the lawyer. Moreover, Jesus did not give the nationality of the wounded man so that any nationality may be meant. Whoever needs our help is our neighbor and whoever helps another is a true neighbor so it works both ways.

It was a masterful presentation of a mighty truth, so skillfully done that the lawyer was obliged to confess the truth so evident. Our Lord then bids him, "Go though and do likewise." The truths of the Word art not merely for reading and inspiration. We are to "go and learn what this meaneth." "Teaching them to observe," not merely to know but to do, is His command. "If ye know these things, happy are ye if ye do them."

"Nothing to Set Before Him"
February 23, 1936

Luke records our Lord's visit in the home of Martha and Mary (10:38-43) where Mary sat at His feet while Martha was unduly worried and taken up with His entertainment. He did not reprove her for working but for worrying. He uses two terms, "Thou art careful and troubled" and we read that she was "cumbered" about much serving. Jesus preferred attention to His teachings to so much fuss and fret about something to eat. Do we not today, in our church activities, spend too much time with secondary busy-ness and not enough at His feet in prayer and worshipful waiting on the Lord?

We read further in this Gospel (11:1-13) that His disciples asked Him, "Lord, teach us to pray, as John also taught his disciples." Not just how to pray but "to pray" which is far better. Some have the theory but still they do not pray! Our Lord gave them what we call the Lord's Prayer, which is His only in the sense that He gave it to us. He never needed to pray it for He had no sins to be forgiven.

It begins with worship and adoration to our Father in Heaven. Then it moves to temporal needs, "our daily bread" and ends with spiritual need, forgiveness and deliverance from evil.

He then tells the parable of the three friends, the friend

who had a friend call upon him at midnight for bread because his friend had come to see him and he had "nothing to set before him." That is the predicament of every one of us in a wider sense. Parents, who are your children but friends come to you in their journey and you have nothing to set before them, you cannot feed their souls unless you borrow loaves from God? Your class at Sunday school, the minister's congregation, your customers in business, all who come to you are your friends come in their journey and you need spiritual bread to set before them. Blessed is the man who knows the way to the Father's house where there is bread to spare. Prayer brings down blessing to pass on. We must come to Him and commune if we are to have anything to communicate.

Jesus here teaches the value of importunate prayer. The request for bread is granted not because the seeker is a friend but because he keeps on asking. So prayer that keeps on never fails. "Ask," that is our Lord's key to spiritual supplies. A for "ask" and S for "seek" and K for "knock." He goes on to say that if earthly fathers give good gifts to their children, how much more will God? I think we often pray as though God were more or less disinterested and we had to coax and persuade Him into helping us. But He is far more anxious to help us than we to be helped. Here He says the Father will give the Spirit to those who ask Him. That is better than to give us things for what we need most is not more things but more of His Spirit by which we can do all things. His strength which is made perfect in weakness.

"Denouncing the Pharisees"
March 1, 1936

Luke records our Lord's burning denunciation of Pharasaism (11:37-54). Invited out to dine He observes no nicety of etiquette but condemns the external formalism of His host and all like-minded who put great care on the externals of religion but whose hearts were "full of ravening and wickedness." Those who are only the meek and gentle side of our Lord should balance that with His fearless attack on the religiousness of His day.

Would He not say the same today in many churches where we go through all the motions, tithe and prayer and seek upper seats, honor God with our lips while our hearts are far from Him? For Pharasaism calls itself by different names but it is still here. Jesus had no soft-tongued tolerance for such hypocrisy and neither should we if we love Him. There is much loose thinking going the rounds today under the guise of tolerance and broad-mindedness that needs to remember 2 John 10,11, where we are commanded not even to receive into our houses those who teach false doctrine.

Of course we must remember the other side expressed in Mk. 9:38-40 where we learn not to condemn others working in His name. Between these two poles the Christian must stand.

Jesus also rebuked the lawyers, that is, those versed in

the Mosaic law, who cluttered it up with their interpretations and kept it not themselves. How true-to-life today is that practice. He condemned of building sepulchers for prophets whom their fathers slew. We condemn God's prophets while they live and succeeding generations honor them. We cast stones at them but our children pick up the stones and build monuments to their honor!

The Lord accused these lawyers of taking away the key of knowledge. Supposed to know the law, they kept it not and, knowing the prophecies, they refused to see Christ as the fulfillment and hindered those who would. What a heavy condemnation rests today upon those who are teachers of the Word and yet do not believe its truths and hinder others by their own unbelief and false teaching.

We read that such withering denunciation incensed the scribes and Pharisees and led them to try to provoke the Lord. He did not deal with them gently. Nowhere in the Gospels does He take any other attitude but that they are blind leaders of the blind and are to be let alone, having sinned against the Holy Ghost. Like Ephraim, they were joined to idols and our Lord knew they could not be won so He ever reproved them and sentenced them to judgment. Their counterpart in any age has always opposed the true work of Christ even while using Christian phraseology and claiming to reverence His name. Our Lord condemned both Pharasaism, lifeless orthodoxy, and Sadduccism, Spiritless liberalism. The modern prophet can do no less and be true to his Lord.

"Thou Fool, This Night"
March 8, 1936

The first portion of Luke 12 records diverse admonitions of our Lord climaxing in the parable of the rich fool. In the presence of a multitude so enormous that men trode upon each other He warned His disciples of the leaven of Pharisaic hypocrisy. Why be hypocritical? All will be revealed anyway so why hide anything? God is presented here sternly as having power to kill and to cast into hell; He is the One to fear.

But He moves immediately to declare that even the sparrows are not forgotten of our Father. Two sparrows are sold for a farthing and five sparrows for two farthings and He is the "God of the odd sparrow." Then, even more minute a figure is used, "even the very hairs of your head are numbered."

Our Lord declares that those who confess Him before men He will confess before the angels and those who deny Him He will deny. We tell people to believe and certainly they must but we have soft-pedaled confession. Yet God's Word couples mouth confession with heart belief in an unmistakable and unbreakable connection (Rom. 10:9, 10). The Bible demands public mouth confession of Christ as Lord and Savior as emphatically as heart belief for salvation.

Jesus presents here the sin of blasphemy against the

Holy Ghost, the sin without forgiveness. It is that expression of a nature so hardened in sin and impervious to God as to call the works of Christ the works of the devil. He advises His disciples not to prepare their messages in advance when called before the synagogues and authorities but to depend upon the Holy Spirit. While this does not rule out sermon preparation it does remind us that humble dependence upon the Spirit is the best rule of homiletics.

The parable of the rich fool was an answer to a covetous request from a man who wanted property. Our Lord first made it clear that He was no judge and divider settling petty differences about lands and goods. "A man's life consisteth not in the abundance of the things which he possesseth." The things may be abundant but the life is not.

The awful contrast appears in the rich fool saying to his soul, "Thou fool, this night..." "We think to make ourselves secure for the future by barricading with stocks and bonds and early wealth but the only life insurance is saving faith in Christ. How foolish that a man will insure life, home, car, everything except his soul, the only thing he will have a few years from now! Men pride themselves on business shrewdness and clever management and fail to receive eternal life. Any man who lets Jesus pass by is a fool, however he rates at the bank. "So is he that layeth up treasure for himself and is not rich toward God."

"Except Ye Repent"
March 22, 1936

We have almost forgotten that repentance is necessary to salvation. In this superficial day, when people glibly "accept Christ" and join the church on a "decision day" with no sense of sin or joy in salvation the depths having never been stirred, we need to remember the words of our Lord, "Except ye repent, ye shall all likewise perish."

In the thirteenth chapter of Luke our Lord mentions two disasters of that time in which a number had been killed. It was the common opinion that such people were greater sinners than the average to bring down such calamity upon themselves. But our Lord declares that "there is no difference." All are sinners and unless we repent we shall all alike perish.

We have our own way of reckoning one man a worse sinner than another, but in God's sight we are all lost until we are saved, and if a man is lost, he cannot be more lost than another. If you are not a believer on Christ, you need not be any worse than you are right now to be lost, for it is your believing that condemns you. (John 3:18.)

Jesus told a parable of a barren fig tree, whose owner was about to destroy it, when the vinedresser interceded to give it another chance. He was speaking of the Jews, typified in Scripture by the fig tree, who had the opportunity for the Messiah's ministry, but had not received Him. It should also remind us that God is giving us an opportunity to bear fruit unto Him, and He wants fruit, not mere leaves of profession.

He healed a crippled woman on the Sabbath, and immediately the Pharisees objected. Jesus sternly calls His accuser a hypocrite and rebukes him. He speaks of the woman as one "whom Satan hath bound" which throws light upon His attitude toward sickness as a shackle of Satan. Often we regard sickness as the will of God when we ought to face it as a scourge of the devil.

When He was asked whether few would be saved (Luke 13:23) He did not answer directly, but bade His hearers to strive to enter in at the strait gate. Many who were highly favored will be cast out while the babes and simple souls will be saved. It has ever been so: the privileged Jews first refused Him while the untaught Gentiles received Him. Through the ages the first have been last and the last first.

When warned that Herod would kill Him, our Lord replies by calling the king a fox and telling him that He could not be hindered by any king. Jesus adds a statement of awful irony about Jerusalem, "I must get on to Jerusalem for it is unthinkable that a prophet should be killed elsewhere. They have killed so many there that it is natural to expect it."

He closes with a lament over the city that He fain would have gathered unto Himself. One day He will return and Israel shall look upon Him whom they have pierced and shall say, "Blessed is he that cometh in the name of the Lord." Today, the papers tell us of continuous return to Palestine and the revival of that land, the greatest miracle of modern times. The stage is being set for the Lord's return. Are you ready?

February 19, 1939

One of those colorful pictures from our Lord's ministry that carries many human interest elements is found in Luke 13:10-17. The Lord was teaching on the Sabbath in one of the synagogues. The day of worship found Him at the house of the Lord. He was not one of those whose manner is to forsake the assembling of themselves, together with other believers on a pretext of worshiping in the great outdoors.

He found in His audience a woman afflicted with a spirit of infirmity bowed together for 18 years. I am struck with the phrase "spirit of infirmity." Our Lord went on to say later that it was Satan who had bound her. There are thousands today shackled with a spirit of infirmity, bound by Satan. Some are not really sick, organically, but bound in mind by fears and obscure mental conditions. They think they are sick and they need the liberating touch of the Lord.

Jesus healed this woman and immediately she was made straight and glorified God. It must have been an exciting time. The man who finds himself released from a spirit of infirmity has a right to praise God and he may be disturbing nuisance to the dignified but God is pleased with the praise of His creatures.

It seems almost incredible that anyone should have complained at such an occurrence but the ruler of the synagogue was angry because Jesus had healed on the Sabbath.

Imagine a soul so warped that it can overlook the loosing of a body bound 18 years and see only the breaking of a custom. But these are still among us. If a revival should break out in the average church today and the hallelujahs of souls set free resound through the house of God, the Pharisees would still object and be more concerned for the infraction of a custom than the freeing of a soul.

Our Lord answered this man by calling him a hypocrite and citing that the law allowed the loosing of an ox or ass to lead it to water. Surely then this poor woman could be loosed from her infirmity on the Sabbath day. Jesus looked over everything else to see human need. He was interested in helping souls, not in observing customs. The Sabbath was made for man and not man for the Sabbath and He used the less to serve the greater.

The adversaries were ashamed, we read, and all the people rejoiced. There has never been a great spiritual movement that did not stir up the opposition of the rulers of the synagogue. The great reformers and preachers of the past have had to contend with the contemporary preachers of their day, the established customs of their times. Finney was reviled because of his new measures. Wesley and Whitefield met the scorn of established religion. Spurgeon was ridiculed as a wild sensationalist. But the common people have heard them gladly and have rejoiced at the power of God shown through them. He who would walk in the steps of the Lord and give himself to loosening the spirit of infirmity in men and women must expect to displease the rulers of the synagogue but he will find the poor and weak and despised praising God for him.

"I and My Father Are One"
March 29, 1936

At the feast of dedication the Jews asked Jesus to declare plainly whether He be the Christ. He answered in effect: "I have told you and you do not believe. My works also prove Who I am but you do not believe because you are not my sheep. My sheep know me, to those who believe I am precious. I give them eternal life and no man can pluck them out of my Father's hand." Here is the security of the believer for all time!

Our Lord then declared, "I and my Father are one." Modernists have toned down this claim of Christ but it was such a tremendous statement that the Jews tried to stone Him for it. They recognized what some do not see today, that Jesus was making Himself God. Our Lord used the Scriptures to show them that even judges were called gods in the Old Testament (Ex. 22:28; Ps. 82:6) and how much more is it the right of God's Son!

Jesus attended the house of a chief Pharisee and healed a man of dropsy (Lk. 14:1-14). It was on the Sabbath and again our Lord put human welfare above prejudices that allowed assistance to an animal on the Sabbath but complained at the healing of a man.

At this dinner there was no doubt, the usual scramble for preferred seats and Jesus gave them the parable of the evil of taking the higher seats only to be sent lower. The core of it is in the final words: "Whosoever exalteth himself shall be abased and he that humbles himself shall be exalted." There is still the scramble for preferred posts even in the churches. The world's philosophy is "Exalt yourself" but our business as Christians is not self-expression but Christ expression. We must decrease that He may increase. We are but the friends of the Bridegroom whose joy should be in hearing the Bridegroom's voice.

Our Lord went on to advise His hosts to make a supper for those who could not repay them in kind. We usually give to those from whom we hope to receive but so did the Pharisees and if your righteousness is to exceed theirs we must go the second mile and give to the unthankful or to those who cannot give in return.

He next gave the parable of the great supper with the trivial excuses of the invited. Notice, even our Lord could give no sensible excuse for not being saved for there is none. First the rulers, then the common people, then Gentiles seem to be implied also in the three groups (Lk. 14:1-24).

Great crowds followed Jesus (Lk. 14:25-35) but He laid down severe terms of absolute surrender and advised them to count the cost. Most of them were superficial disciples for at Pentecost we find only a hundred and twenty. He wants us to know what we are doing. He will have no glib acceptance based on momentary enthusiasm. There is much salt without savor today, empty profession without the needed possession.

"When a Man Comes to Himself"
April 5, 1936

In the fifteenth chapter of Luke our Lord gives the parable of the lost sheep, the lost coin, and the lost son. It has been pointed out that the coin was lost and did not know it was lost; the sheep was lost, knew it was lost but did not know the way home, while the prodigal was lost, knew he was lost and knew the way home.

The lost sheep illustrates our Lord's concern for the straying soul. The lost coin illustrates the joy "in the presence of the angels," among the redeemed over one sinner recovered.

Have you noticed how many things the prodigal came to before he came to himself? He came to his father, to the far country, to riotous living, to want, to degradation, all before he came to himself. Sin is a state of departure from God, a spending state, a wanting state. The famine always follows the far country.

This youngster didn't know when he left home that he was headed for a hogpen. He started for pleasure and ended in the pigsty! And what degradation it was for a Jew to be forced to feed hogs!

But he came to himself. The longest road in life is usually the road to one's own self. We come to everything else first. We do everything possible to avoid meeting "old number 1." The jails, asylums, hospitals are filled with people trying to get away from themselves. But around some corner we must run into ourselves.

The prodigal came first to consideration: "How many hired servants of my father's have bread enough and to spare, and I perish with hunger!" He realized that he was in a dissatisfied state. "He would fain have filled himself." He was in a disappointed state: "No man gave unto him." He was in a dead state: "This my son was dead." He was in a demented state for if he came to himself he must have been beside himself.

He came to conviction: "I have sinned." Others said that in the Bible but only David and the prodigal really repented. He came to the decision: "I will arise and go to my father." He did something about it. He could have sat among the hogs the rest of his life feeling sorry but he decided and then acted upon it, he arose and came home. He made confession in all humility and was willing to be made a hired servant. "A broken and a contrite heart, O God, Thou will not despise."

So he came home and "when he was yet a great way off his father saw him." The prodigal did not even finish the speech he had prepared. He was restored and reinstated. The robe speaks of the garments of Christ's righteousness, the ring of our adoption, the shoes of sonship for slaves went barefoot, the fatted calf of the rich satisfactions of the Gospel.

"They began to be merry." We do not read that it stopped. There is joy over the sinner come home and it goes on through all eternity. Take care that you are not a sour, Pharisaic older brother who grows bitter over the joyous delights of others when sinners come home to God.

"Make Friends With Money"
April 12, 1936

One of the strangest of the parables of Jesus is that of the unjust steward (Lk. 16:1-13). Here is a steward about to be turned out of his job who cleverly gets himself into the good graces of debtors to his master by reducing all their accounts. He thus hopes to be welcomed into their homes after he loses his position. And his master commends him, not for his dishonesty but for his foresight in looking after himself.

Our Lord uses this strange story to drive home the point that the people of this world are more prudent in their temporal affairs than believers who are stewards of the manifold grace of God. The proper investment of money is in helping others that when we die they may welcome us to our eternal home. It is plainly taught that those we help here shall greet us in heaven, if they are believers, and that throws light on recognition of friends in heaven. Paul tells us to communicate and lay up in store for ourselves a good foundation against the time to come, that we may lay hold on eternal life (I Tim. 6:18, 19.)

We are bidden to labour, working with our hands the thing which is good, that we may have–not to put away in the bank–but to give to him that needeth (Eph. 4:29.) It is generally overlooked that the Bible teaches that money is to be invested in others where it is sure to pay dividends. If thousands who put it in banks during the past years had put it in human lives they might now be realizing returns.

But our Lord goes even further. He plainly declares (Lk. 16:10-12) that how we handle money is an index to how we would handle greater treasure. If we do not rightly use that which is anothers (for to have is to woe, not own) how shall we use spiritual wealth? I am convinced that God is withholding blessing from many a man today because He has first tried the man out with money and he has not been faithful in that, so He will not commit greater things to his stewardship. If we are unfaithful in the less, we shall surely be in the greater.

The Pharisees derided Jesus for this teaching. They still deride the man today who follows Him in this precept and practice. For Pharisees follow the wisdom of earth and lay up treasure while the Lord bids us to be rich toward God and rich in faith. After all these years of preaching the average Christian follows the world's code in investment of money.

It certainly is a neglected truth that the use we make of money here will have much to do with our heavenly reception when we reach the other side. The greatest fortune is found in friends and the Christian should certainly use spiritual foresight even as this world uses it in things temporal. Make friends with money rightly spent in the Name of the Lord!

"If They Hear Not Moses"
April 19, 1936

In the account of the rich man and Lazarus (Lk. 16:19-31) our Lord evidently had just related the parable of the unjust steward and so here He pressed on to show the need of rightly using wealth in this present world, the folly of gaining the world and losing ones own soul.

Doubtless, He had also in mind the Jewish nation which had refused Him, the haughty Pharisees who rejected the Messiah. Moses and the prophets had testified of Him and if they were not enough they would not be persuaded if one rose from the dead which one did in the case of Lazarus.

Nor can anyone deny, even if it be granted that the main object of this passage is not to teach about hell, that our Lord Himself gave us the most fearful pictures of eternal punishment to be found in the Bible. Here He plainly shows that those in torment have sight, they suffer, they speak, they have memory, they have concern for others. And there is the great gulf fixed. Critics have done their utmost to tone down this picture but our Lord here as well as else held the very opposite of present-day sentimental ideas about hell.

Another truth, usually overlooked in this passage, comes out in the last verse: "If they hear not Moses and the prophets, neither will they be persuaded, though one rose from the dead." It applies first to the Jew of course. Their rejection of the resurrection of Lazarus and our Lord proved that. But it also applies to us. Dives is a type of those today, both sinners and saints, who demand some extra sign in addition to the Word of God. The Bible is not enough for them and they think they would believe if they were furnished some remarkable extra display or manifestation.

Some think that if Christ were walking among us in the flesh more would believe. But in His own day, while multitudes followed Him, most of them were superficial disciples out for the loaves and fishes. Human nature has not changed. Faith that will not depend on His Word would not be convinced by works. If men refuse the Word of God, nothing else will be enough.

Even Christians fall into the error of demanding extra signs, feelings, visions, experiences, to confirm the Word of God. The Word often is not enough for assurance. Like Thomas they demand to see before believing forgetting that our Lord promised the greater blessing to those who see not, yet believe. True, God often favors believers with extra evidences and confirmations of His Word but not because they would not take the bare Word. To ask for further evidence is to doubt God. If Moses and the prophets...and now the whole New Testament...be not enough no other demonstration would be enough. We think it would but it would not. Praise God for the sufficiency of His Word!

"No Joy Allowed"

The triumphant entry of our Lord into Jerusalem (Luke 19:29-44) and the subsequent cleansing of the temple abound in lessons for the individual heart and the church. Christ must first enter the heart as King through acceptance by faith. As many as receive Him receive power to become the sons of God, even them that believe on His name. And this coming of Jesus into the heart means joy. We read that when He entered Jerusalem the disciples began to "rejoice and praise God with a loud voice for all the mighty works that they had seen." Of course the Pharisees objected and asked the Lord to rebuke His disciples but He answered, "I tell you that if these should hold their peace, the stones would immediately cry out."

The church today suffers with a joyless experience. Christ is not joyfully acclaimed as King. A noiseless religion is the order of the day, no shouting, no amens, no hallelujahs. If some brother does occasionally grow happy, there is a wail from the Pharisees. But our Lord approved it and still does. When He enters a heart to reign, if ever there was something to rejoice about certainly that ought to set the joybells ringing.

We still have the same types and classes that existed in our Lord's day. We call them by different names but the Pharisees, the Sadducees, the common people, the lame and sick, the disciples, are with us. You will observe that our Lord dealt with them in different ways.

After entering Jerusalem as King, He next cleansed the temple. When He enters the heart, He next cleanses it. He is priest as well as king. The church needs a mighty cleansing for it has become a den of thieves today. So do our bodies the temples of the Holy Spirit.

Then we read that the blind and lame came to Him and He healed them. To those who would desecrate God's house, He brought a rod of anger but to the needy he was love and tenderness. Once again there was joy for we read that the little children were crying "Hosanna to the son of David" and the Pharisees were sore displeased. They asked Him, "Hearest Thou what these say?" It was too much emotionalism, too sensational for the temple! But our Lord replied, "Yea; have ye never read, out of the mouth of babes and sucklings thou hast perfected praise?"

It has ever been thus. God's secrets have been kept from the wise and prudent and revealed unto babes. It is the child-like who enter the kingdom (Mat. 18:3). And when these simple-hearted believers begin to rejoice, the Pharisees always grumble. The note of joy has gone from our churches. It had been so long since there had been rejoicing in the old temple that the Pharisees were horrified. If somebody would grow happy today in some of these molded and musty churches, it would startle some of the old bench-warmers out of their wits. There couldn't be less rejoicing in many of our churches today if "No Joy Allowed" were on the door as you enter.

His entrance and cleansing still bring joy. When Philip preached in Samaria, there was an exciting time with demons coming out and souls being saved. I read "there was great joy in that city. It has always been so and we shall never see sinners converted until the lost joy of salvation is restored."

"Christ the Opener"
April 29, 1934

The twenty-fourth chapter of Luke tells the sweet story of the appearance of our Lord to the two disciples on the way to Emmaus. They were trudging along, half-believing, half-doubting, communing together and reasoning, which never amounts to anything without our Lord's Presence. He draws near and begins to talk with them, drawing them out first, then showing them how He was fulfilling the Scriptures.

In this chapter our Lord starts out as the Great Opener. First, He opened to them the Scriptures and their hearts burned within them (v. 32). God's Word, rightly interpreted, will produce spiritual heart-burn. It penetrates for it is sharper than a two-edged sword (Heb.4:12). Believers do not hunger and thirst after righteousness because they do not read God's Word. They fill up with the lollipops of this world and have no appetite for spiritual things. They do not read their Bibles nor go to a church where the Scriptures are really opened and they are not smitten with spiritual heart-burn and a yearning for a deeper life. If we will give Christ an opportunity to open to us His Word our hearts will burn and we will cry, "Abide with us for it is toward evening and the day is far spent." To be sure, He dwells in every believer's heart after regeneration but we need to cry out,

"Abide with me in a deeper consciousness of Thy Presence."

We observe next that, while Jesus sat at meat with them, "their eyes were opened and they knew Him" (v. 31). Up until then, their eyes were holden (v. 16) and they did not know Him. So many believers walk with a veiled Christ for their eyes are holden. They need that their eyes shall be fully opened to know Him and, while they may be seeking some spectacular experience, they need to remember that He was revealed here in the very lowliest way, "in breaking of bread" (v. 35). Perhaps you want Him to dazzle you with a mighty vision when He wants you to know Him as the other member of your family in the kitchen and as your partner in the office.

Finally, we notice in verse 45 that "He opened their understanding that they might understand the Scriptures." First, He opened the Scriptures, then their eyes and then their understanding that they might understand the Scriptures for themselves. It is the Divine order. It is fellowship with the Lord, and not scholarship, that opens to us the Word. Colleges cannot do it, seminaries cannot do it, seminaries cannot do it, He must do it. There are clever theologians who can divide the Word but they cannot rightly divide it until He has opened their eyes to the knowledge of Himself. This explains why so many scholars are dry and some simple souls have such a grasp of the Bible, there is a key to it that hangs low and only the lowly stoop to find it.

Many read the Bible but need to be asked, as was the eunuch, "Understandeth thou what thou readest?" The best way–the only way–to know the Bible is first to know its Christ. The Scriptures may be opened to bring conviction and heartburn as here but, until the eyes have been opened, teaching deep things of the Word to those with holden eyes is casting pearls before swine. "The natural man receiveth not the things of the Spirit of God," there must be a miracle.

"Christ the Opener"

"Open thou mine eyes that I may behold wondrous things out of thy law" (Ps. 119:18) is the only true approach to understanding the Scriptures.

February 26, 1939

In Luke 24:44-49 our Lord gave to His disciples, just before He ascended to the Father, a precious summary of Gospel truth.

He began: "These are the words which I spake unto you while I was yet with you, that all things must be fulfilled, which are written in the law of Moses, and in the prophets, and in the psalms, concerning me." Here is the fulfilment of prophecy and notice how He includes the whole of the Old Testament Scriptures, the law, the psalms, the prophets. For a right view of the Gospel we must start with Genesis. After He said this, we read that "then opened He their understanding that they might understand the scriptures." "Faith cometh by hearing and hearing by the Word of God" and our Lord is the true key to the Scriptures.

He said next, "Thus it is written and thus it behoved Christ to suffer and to rise from the dead the third day." The Gospel begins with "It is written," it is a revelation of God and is built upon recorded facts in His Word. And the twin Gospel facts are the death and resurrection of our Lord. So Paul made it in 1 Cor. 15:3,4. So it is declared in Romans 4:25, "Delivered for our offences and raised for our justification." So does baptism set forth the twin facts of our death with Christ to sin and our resurrection to walk in newness of life. Calvary and the open tomb must always go together.

With these two glorious facts to proclaim, our Lord said next "that repentance and remission of sins should be preached in His name among all nations, beginning at Jerusalem." Remission of sins is made possible through His shed blood but before it can become effectually ours, there must be repentance, a change of mind about sin, self and the Savior and a turning from darkness to light. The repentance note has been left out of much of our preaching. It is primary to point out the blessed grace of God with pardon offered freely to all but God commandeth all men everywhere to repent and we dare not do less.

"And ye are witnesses of these things." Witnesses of His death and resurrection. The disciples had seen Him die but all who believe are witnesses of these things in experience. He also said that we are witnesses unto Him but before we can witness to we must be witnesses of these facts in our own lives. We cannot witness to something we know not of. That is the tragedy of much preaching today, it is a speaking about these facts without a warm personal experience of them.

But the weakness in much testimony is implied in our Lord's next word here: "And behold I send the promise of my Father upon you: but tarry ye in the city of Jerusalem, until ye be endued with power from on high." It is not enough even to be witnesses of these facts if we speak them without the power which must accompany them. The early church had the facts but had to wait for the fire. We today need not wait for Pentecost to come but we need to tarry to get right with God and yielded to Him. It is not that He must be coaxed, it is not His reluctance but our rebellion that hinders the blessing.

Putting all these words together we have the Gospel summary: prophecy fulfilled, the Word, Calvary and the resurrection, repentance and remission, witnessing and the power of the Spirit.

PART FOUR

REFLECTIONS ON THE GOSPEL OF JOHN

"A New Life Begun"
March 18, 1934

The eternal life made possible for us through the Lord Jesus Christ is supernatural. It is not an improvement of our best natures nor a refining of the life we already have but a new life altogether and is therefore begun by an inward miracle, a new birth from above.

There are three significant "musts" in the third chapter of John, in verses 7, 14, and 30. They are the musts of the sinner, of the Saviour and of the saint. The Lord told Nicodemus he must be reborn. Some, doubtless, have wished Christ had said that to a more vicious sinner than Nicodemus, a teacher, moral, respectable, honored and earnestly seeking light. But Christ said it to this prominent and noble character that no man might think he did not need regeneration. If Nicodemus needed it, certainly we do.

The necessity of the new birth arises from the fact that "the natural man receiveth not the things of the Spirit of God; for they are foolishness unto him: neither can he know them, because they are spiritually discerned" (1 Cor. 2:14). However educated, talented and moral, the ordinary powers of human nature cannot receive the new life of God so the implantation of a new nature is necessary. "The carnal mind is enmity against God: for it is not subject to the law of God, neither indeed can be. So then they that are in the flesh cannot please God" (Rom. 8:7,8). This is parallel with what our Lord told Nicodemus: "that which is born of the flesh is flesh; and that which is born of the Spirit is spirit." So this eternal life of God must be born in us by the operation of the Spirit through the consent of our wills and our faith in Jesus Christ. "As many as received Him...were born, not of blood, nor of the will of the flesh, nor of the will of man, but of God" (John 1:12, 13).

The new birth is not preached now as of old because men have changed their concept of the life which Christ offers us. He has become merely an example of faith instead of the object of faith and His life has become merely the limitation of His character and the observance of His ideals. Since He has been brought down from the supernatural in common thinking, men do not think a supernatural change is necessary to share His life. So the improvement of the old nature has taken the place of the Divine impartation of a new nature.

But human nature has never been able to produce one Christian because, however it may strain to be something else, flesh remains flesh. Certain commendable traits may be developed, virtues assumed, and even an impressive character built up by will power and idealism but it is built and not grown, it has not the life of Christ in it.

How is the new life begun? There is mystery involved to be sure. God's side is regeneration and we cannot understand that. Our side is to realize that we are flesh and sinners, to turn from sin and receive the Lord Jesus Christ by faith. When we thus repent, turn and believe, God works within us the miracle whereby His life enters our own and we become partakers of His nature. That His purpose with us is that this new life might fill every part of our being, might become our only interest, that the old nature may recede, Christ increase and self decrease until we can say "to me to live is Christ."

It is new life we need and life can be begun only by birth and the new life by the new birth.

"Come and See"
March 17, 1935

John the Baptist stood with his disciples and declared Jesus to be the Lamb of God. John's other statements about our Lord were in terms of His Messiahship but this, with Isa. 53:7 in mind, looks toward Calvary.

When two of John's disciples began to follow the Lord, He enquired, "What seek ye?" What do we seek in Him today? And what do we seek in life? They asked where He dwelt. That is life's supreme issue, not where dwells this or that thing we seek but where does He dwell Who is Life and Truth?

The answer, given to these and later by Phillip to Nathanael, is the very heart of the Christian experience: "Come and see." If you would know the truth about our Lord, it cannot be reached by argument and speculation. "Come and see," that is the road to certainty. "If any man will to do His will he shall know of the doctrine, whether it be of God or whether I speak of myself."

One of the two, Andrew, went for his brother Simon. That is a true mark of discipleship, that we seek our brother. And he brought him to Jesus. No greater thing Andrew ever did for his Lord. If you are not an "important" disciple as Peter was you can be Andrew.

Next Philip followed, then went after Nathanael

(Bartholomew.) What a testimony to bring, that he had found the long-expected Messiah! Nathanael is disposed to raise questions but Philip offers the practical test: Come and see. He wisely did not argue the question of whether any good thing could come out of Nazareth. Don't argue secondary issues with questioners: tell them to come and see, Christ is Himself the answer to their doubts.

Our Lord knew Nathanael in advance as a devout Israelite. He knew the hours Nathanael had spent under the fig tree. God knows our hearts, our tears, the secret prayers, the longings of the soul, of which men know nothing. He knows the long, lean years when we prayed and seemed to receive nothing. How it must have seemed sometimes to Nathanael that the Messiah would never come! Don't give up the fig tree! He sees you through the tedious, commonplace years and one day your great moment will come and you shall cry out as Nathanael: "Thou are the Son of God; Thou art the King of Israel." He will reveal Himself to the faithful.

And not only that but we shall see greater things than these! For there is greater glory ever to be revealed and what we see here is but the foretaste of more to follow. As Jesus told Nathanael, He is the Jacob's ladder between earth and heaven. Jacob learned at Bethel that all heaven was interested in him. So angels are our ministers (Heb. 1:14) and our Lord Himself is the ladder ("ascending and descending upon the Son of man.")

So Nathanael's experience had three stages. First, the long years of prayer and waiting. Then the revelation of the Lord. And the rest of his life and increasing fellowship with heaven through Christ. Truly if we "come and see" we shall "see greater things than these."

"Three 'Musts' of John 3"
June 6, 1937

The word "must" is surely unpopular nowadays. Neither children nor adults like to be told what they must do. Yet there are certain compulsions in God's Word and there is no way around them. They must be met if we are going to obey God.

Three of these "musts" occur in John 3. There is one for the sinner, one for the Saviour and one for the saint.

There is first the compulsion of conversion: "Ye must be born again" (Verse 7). There must be a new life if we are to be saved for the old life ends in physical and spiritual death. "That which is born of the flesh is flesh" and "they that are in the flesh cannot please God" for "the carnal mind is enmity against God." The only way to get into the kingdom of God is to be born into it. One cannot merely take naturalization papers and get in! One may learn French, live in France, speak French and still not be a Frenchman. So one may know doctrine and work in the church but not be a Christian. It takes more than knowing the Constitution to make one an American and it takes more than knowing theology to be a Christian.

The new birth is mysterious (John 3:7,8); it is the work of the Holy Spirit using the word (Titus 3:5; Jas. 1:18; 1 Pt. 1:23): On our part, the means is faith (Gal. 3:26). The new birth is manifested in a new creation (2 Cor. 5:17; love 1 John 3:14; 4:7; victory over sin (1 John 3:9; 5:18); righteous living (1 John 2:29; overcoming the world (1 John 5:4.)

Then there is the compulsion of Calvary: "As Moses lifted up the serpent in the wilderness, even so must the Son of man be lifted up" (Verse 14). If we must be born again, there must be a way provided by which to receive eternal life. So God sent His only begotten Son. If there could have been salvation some other way, God would have been cruel to choose the way of the cross. But it behooved Christ to suffer and He Himself said, "Ought not Christ to have suffered these things?" (Lk. 24:26). If it was so important that Christ had to die, then woe unto us if we disregard it!

Finally, there is the compulsion of consecration: John the Baptist said, "He must increase, but I must decrease" (Verse 30). The believer must die to self, reckon himself dead indeed unto sin, deny himself, count himself crucified with Christ that Christ may fill his life and be all in all. The Christian is only the friend of the bridegroom and his delight is in hearing the bridegroom's voice. This means more than the mere giving up of amusements, money, time: it means renouncing one's own will and self. Peter forsook his nets and boat on his first call; it was quite a while before he gave up himself.

Said George Muller: "There was a day when I died, utterly died to George Muller, his opinions, preferences, will, died to the world, its approval or censure." Luther used to smite his breast and say, "Martin Luther does not live here: Jesus Christ lives here."

These are God's compulsions. Between conversion and consecration stands Christ and He is the key to both. We are saved by simple believing and receiving Him; we are consecrated as we yield to Him and are able to say, "Not I, but Christ."

"John 3:16"
January 2, 1938

"For God so loved the world that He gave His only begotten Son that whosoever believeth in Him should not perish, but have everlasting life."

Here indeed is the "little Bible" that contains the whole Gospel. And it begins with God as the Bible begins. There is much talk nowadays about Christocentric, Christ-centered, preaching which falls short of the mark. The plan of salvation begins not with Christ but with God and His holiness, then sin and man's lost state. There is much superficial "believing in Jesus" that has never faced sin, that professes but never possesses eternal life.

David cried to God, "Against Thee, Thee only, have I sinned." There must first be conviction of sin, that we face a holy and just God Who demands a fixed standard of righteousness which we cannot reach. Then we are ready to look to Jesus, Who became sin for us that we might have this righteousness which is Christ Himself. But we must start with God.

"For God so loved the world." He hates sin but loves the sinner. Do not think of Calvary in this light that God was angry at the human race and Jesus had to die to put Him in a god humor. I have heard preaching that amounts to that. Rather it was God Himself Who so loved us that He sent His

Son. While we make much of Calvary as Christ's suffering—and we cannot make too much of that—let us think of God's own suffering heart. Calvary was not only a revelation of the love of the Son but of the Father's love. In His earthly life, our Lord kept giving God the glory, lest men forget God and see only Jesus.

"For God so loved the world." That word "so" is one of the mightiest in all speech. God had sent His servants the prophets and then He said, "Maybe they will reverence my Son." If you love your son as you do, think of how much the heart of God must have loved His only Son. And He just "gave" Him; there were no "strings" to it.

"That whosoever believeth in Him should not perish but have everlasting life." There are two alternatives, live or perish. Eternal decay is here declared, that eternal decay of the soul in the lake of fire prefigured by the valley of Hinnom where worms work in putrefying carcasses and the smoke of burning ever rises. "Except ye repent, ye shall all likewise perish." But there is also eternal life, not merely in the matter of length and duration but because it is the very life of God. God's life offered to us through His Son. And it is available to whosoever believeth regardless of color or standing. The only requirement is faith, active faith that receives the Son into the heart. Some time ago, a man objected that he could not believe. "Why," said the minister who was dealing with him, "I understand that some time ago you believed the prospectus of a wildcat oil company and you lost plenty of money." Men will believe the most ridiculous things, but they reject God's own word. "He that believeth on Him is not condemned; but he that believeth not is condemned already," not because he has robbed a bank or done some other terrible crime, but "because he hath not believed in the name of the only begotten Son of God." You use your will against Him and you can use it for Him. "Whosoever will let him come."

"Condemned"
April 22, 1937

"He that believeth on Him is not condemned: but he that believeth not is condemned already, because he hath not believed in the name of the only begotten Son of God."–John 3:18.

Someone has said that, whatever has happened to other wages, there has been a reduction in the wages of sin. Of course he meant that judgement and hell and the wrath of God are not being preached as once they were. Millions regard hell as a superstition, the judgment as a myth. Thousands of church-members do not believe in eternal punishment or doubt it, to say the least. Such an attitude is not a sign of intelligence but of stupidity. When God has spoken on a subject as plainly as He has on this, then the man who shuts his eyes and stops his ears to it is a fool.

God has said that the unbeliever is condemned. He shows that he is condemned as John 3:19 declares because he loves darkness rather than light. If you dislike plain preaching it is likely because you are living in darkness and you don't like the Gospel searchlight. When the straight, undiluted Gospel is being preached and some fellow winces and squirms and twists and goes out to criticize nine times out of ten he is living in condemnation and dreads the light. On the other hand, a righteous man seeks the light and wants to know the truth and desires that God should search him and know his heart and try him and know his thoughts.

What is this condemnation? It is God's sentence upon sin, the second death, eternal separation from God in hell. God is love but He is also a consuming fire and it is a fearful thing to fall into the hands of the living God.

Who is condemned? He who does not believe. I care not what street he lives on, what car he drives, or the size of his salary. He may belong to "Who's Who" and "What's What" but God has only one yardstick and he that does not believe on Christ with a living, saving faith, whether rich man, poor man, beggar man or thief, is condemned already. He may be an upstanding and outstanding citizen, active in church-work and belonging to all the idealistic clubs in town and have a high moral character and a spotless reputation but if he believes not of the saving of the soul he is in the gall of bitterness and the bond of iniquity and the wrath of God abides upon him.

When is he condemned? Already, not tomorrow, not at death or the judgment, not maybe, possibly, but he is condemned now and is merely waiting to begin serving his sentence.

Why is he condemned? It is stated twice in our text. He that believeth not is condemned already because he hath not believed on the name of the only begotten Son of God. Not because he robbed a bank or killed somebody but because he has not believed. When we think of condemned people, we think of gangsters and kidnapers but any man who does not believe is condemned.

How shall we escape condemnation? By believing, of course, and receiving the Lord Jesus as Savior. He who hears and believe shall not come into condemnation. (John 5:24) there is no condemnation to them which are in Christ Jesus (Rom. 8:1). Believe Him and rest upon His finished work and as surely as once you were condemned so surely will you be saved.

"The Increasing Christ"
October 1932

I have long been impressed with the thirtieth verse of the third chapter of John. Some of the disciples of John the Baptist come to him reporting that everybody has gone after Jesus; the Baptist has been eclipsed, his popularity has passed its peak. But the rugged old prophet graciously replies in part "He must increase, but I must decrease."

Nothing is more needed among Christians than the lesson of the decreasing self. It is an ego-centric age, a day of self-sufficiency. The world's creed, is "Glorify Yourself," "Express Yourself." And just as a penny held close to the eye will hide the sun, so does the penny of self shut out God.

Several years ago, walking along the rim of the Grand Canyon, I came upon a girl reading a novel! With such a masterpiece of God to look at, what a place to be reading a novel! Yet, how many of us miss the far-flung horizons of the life that is bid with Christ in God, absorbed with the pitiful things of self.

Some one has pointed out that the word "sin" revolves as upon a pivot around the central letter "i." Verily, sin does revolve around I–self. That was the trouble with the Rich Fool: "This I will do: I will pull down my barns and build greater; and there will I bestow all my fruits and my goods.

And I will say to my soul" etc,–notice the "I's" and "my's". The Pharisee praying in the parable of Jesus was another of the same sort: "God, I thank thee that I am not as other men." Both had I–trouble, they were self-centered.

    The business of the Christian is to express Christ. To do that, he must decrease and Christ must increase. As at Cana, it is only when the wine of our won self-sufficiency gives out that we get the better wine which Christ provides. There must be the emptying of self if there is to be His infilling. Paul speaks of "Having nothing, yet possessing all things." One must come first to the first half of that phrase and realize his own nothingness before he truly can appropriate that other verse of Paul's: "All things are yours."

> "All of self and none of Thee!
> Some of self and some of Thee!
> Less of self and more of Thee!
> None of self and all of Thee!"

    We ought to be careful how we endorse the world's creed of self-glorification. Magazines are full of self-development propaganda. Inspirational speakers fads and isms tell us of our latent powers that can make giants of weaklings. Of course, there is a sense in which we must make the most of our personal capital as stewards of God but one easily can drift here into self-sufficiency. God's strength is made perfect in our weakness and Paul said when he was weak he was strong. This is distasteful doctrine to a humanistic age that feels so need of the supernatural. One is a good Christian in proportion as he reveals Jesus rather than himself. When one buys a glass for a picture he is not interested so much in the beauty of the glass as in how well it reveals the picture. The real test of a Christian is his spiritual transparency. Billy Sunday well said "we put such a big 'I' in front of the cross that the sinner can't see Jesus."

"The Increasing Christ"

The world asks "Are you growing bigger?" Christ asks "Are you growing less?" Paul was a self-sufficient man on the Damascus road that morning. But with his conversion a new process began, his en-Christment. The longer he lived the less there was of Paul and the more there was of Christ until he could say "Not I but Christ who liveth in me: and "To me to live is Christ."

"He must increase; we must decrease."

"At Jacob's Well"
June 19, 1938

The account of our Lord's interview with the woman at Jacob's well carries many precious truths which we might easily overlook. Our Lord was on a detour here and we observe that some of our best work is often done off the main line. No one knew what the good Samaritan had started out to do that day but he is remembered for what he did not start out to do. Bunyan wrote Pilgrim's Progress as a sort of matter on the side but by it he is remembered.

Our Lord first broke custom by speaking to the Samaritan woman. We need to shatter precedent and must if we are to win souls. This woman knew only the well of Jacob. How many souls are depending today upon broken cisterns that can hold no water and know not the gift of God!

This woman was disposed to raise side issues but our Lord brought the matter down to the sin in her life: "Go, call thy husband..." Immediately the woman said, "Sir, I perceive that Thou art a prophet." The mark of a prophet is to bring people to realize they are sinners. Too much preaching today never exposes sin, never makes people face their iniquities. This woman kept speaking to Jesus as the one who told her all things that ever she did. She so described Him to her acquaintance back in the city. There is a pleasant preaching today that tries to prescribe the remedy before people are made to realize that they are sick, tries to lead to the light people who do not know they are in the dark. Men will never be convicted until they are made to see themselves sinners and to do that, sin must be condemned and exposed and it must be made personal. We must get down to the street where people live. Jesus did not give this woman a lecture on sin in general. He spoke of her sin. Romans starts by picturing sin and it names sins and then proclaims the remedy in justification by faith.

When you get close to the sins of people, do not be surprised if they want to change the subject. This woman immediately raised the issue of where to worship. How easily sinners shift the subject of conversation when you specify sins in their lives! But our Lord was not to be sidetracked, He held to the subject.

Finally when she spoke of the coming Messiah, our Lord made clear and unmistakable claim to be the One Who should come. It is strange how any one can read our Lord's claim here and then deny that He ever professed to be the Messiah.

The woman left her waterpots and went into the city to tell others of this prophet she had found. When we find the Living Water, we have no more use of the broken cisterns of earth. She was a good personal worker for she brought her crowd back with her to see the Lord.

The disciples who had been out looking for meat came back and marveled at our Lord's conversation with this woman. They were looking for meat. He was looking for men. The church today is too busy looking for tangible things, numbers, money, success. If we made our business soul-wining which is the business of the church, all other things would be added.

"At Jacob's Well"
April 14, 1935

Our Lord must needs go through Samaria. Our by-way ministries often are more fruitful than our service on the main road. "Being wearied with His journey" our Lord sat on the well. It is a precious human touch.

Then follows a masterpiece of personal work. This woman, coming at noon to draw water, was a bad character. But our Lord saw a soul to save. We love to preach but do we love the people to whom we preach? We still snub the Samaritans and need to read James 2:1-9.

"If thou knewest the gift of God, and who it is that saith to thee, Give me to drink; thou wouldest have asked of him and he would have given thee living water." If only men knew the gift of God and the Giver; the water here points to John 6:37-39 where we know the Lord speaks of the Spirit.

The woman asks whether our Lord is greater than Jacob. The well is deep and He has nothing to draw with; How we let trifling circumstances stand between us and Him! And how we cling to Jacob rather than Jesus! We measure our lives by the things we get from Jacob, by inheritance or circumstance. We cling as in Jer. 2:13 to broken cisterns but here is one greater than Jacob who can give us living water shall thirst again!" The water of Jacob's well never satisfies.

When the woman makes a light reply, our Lord strikes at

the real problem in her life: "Go, call thy husband." Sin always lies at the base of scepticism. "We are not sinners because we are skeptics but skeptics because we are sinners."

The woman again side-steps with another issue about where to worship but our Lord meets it with the declaration of true worship "in spirit and in truth." Then comes a clear claim to be the Messiah and the woman leaves her waterpots to go tell others. When we come to know Him we shall leave our waterpots which we have carried to Jacob's well! The old things are deserted, the water or the natural cannot meet our need, we have found living water!

This woman was a true soul-winner, she told others and brought others to Jesus. Thus they came to know Him for themselves and not only through another. "We have heard Him ourselves and know that this is indeed the Christ, the saviour of the world." It is the argument of experience.

Our Lord was found by the disciples in this strong interview, astounding to them. Our meat, like His, should be to do the will of God. The world says "Four months and then cometh harvest." We are not concerned for the lost. Likely the Samaritans were coming across the fields as our Lord said: "Lift up your eyes and look on the fields; for they are white already to harvest." That we might see the lost today with the urgency of our Lord! Remember "he that gathereth not with me scattereth abroad."

"Go Thy Way"
April 21, 1935

The healing of the nobleman's son (John 4:43-54) brings to us certain precious truths that apply along the entire range of experience. Our Lord was a prophet without honor in His own country (a statement declared in each of the Gospels) so we may take heart if we fare similarly.

So He comes into Galilee and a nobleman besought him for the healing of his son. Our Lord tests him by saying: "Except ye see signs and wonders, ye will not believe." It is a mark of most of us today that we are "from Missouri" and still demands visible evidences before we believe. How much more blessed, our Lord told Thomas, are they who have not seen, yet believe (John 20:29.)

The man continues to plead for help and Jesus tells him, "Go thy way; thy son liveth." That probably was not the way the man expected it to be done but he believed and went his way and the miracle took place at that moment. There are times when we do not see our prayer answered as we expected, visibly, right before your eyes. We are merely told to go our way and trust God for the rest like the lepers who, as they went, were cleansed (Lk. 17:14.) We wanted things to happen at once but our orders are to go trusting and leave the rest with God. Can you so trust Him, going on when to all appearances nothing has changed "yet believing?"

The nobleman reaches home and finds the wonder wrought and wrought at the same moment that the Lord said, "Go thy way." Observe that we read twice that the nobleman believed, once in verse 50 when our Lord sent him on his way and again in verse 53 when he reached home and found the boy healed. He believed first because of Christ's word as we are plainly told and the second time because of Christ's work. There is a faith that takes God at His word before we see any wonder wrought; then there is a deeper faith, a surety that comes when we behold His work. The first faith depends upon promise; the second grows out of performance. If we have enough faith to do His will we shall know of the doctrine. We shall be as the Samaritans who first believed the word of the woman, then believed upon their own experience (John 4:42.)

I have thought of that nobleman on his way home. What doubts may have assailed him! How he might have said: "Suppose I am mistaken? How do I know this will take place: I certainly do not feel any differently!" It seems hard that our Lord did not go along with this troubled man but He was teaching him to know that to believe is to see. Many times we wish the Lord would "go along" with us when in trouble in some visible sign of His love and care but as with Martha and Mary He tarries in the same place where He is. Ah, it is only that we might know that His Word is enough to go our way upon and that when He gives us His Word He surely will follow it with His work.

Do you believe Him enough to "go your way" though no sign is given, trusting the evidence to await you at the end of the venture of faith rather than at the beginning? Mind you, the miracle was performed when the man believed and so it ever is but the visible evidence often lies further on. Believe the Word and you will believe again in the certainty of His work.

"At the Pool of Bethesda"
June 2, 1935

The impotent man at the pool of Bethesda (John 5) was seeking the best help he could get so far as he knew. Our Lord asked him, "Wilt thou be made whole?" and so does He ask us today for He would give us health of soul. The poor man saw only circumstance as did the woman at Jacob's well (John 4:11), Phillip at the feeding of the multitude (John 6:7) and Martha at Lazarus' grave (John 11.) But He obeyed the Lord's command, arose and walked.

This brought on a storm, with the Jews who could look clear over such a wonderful blessing and see only a breach of the law! Verily their kind are still with us, men who miss blessing to quibble over tradition and custom. Our Lord proceeded to declare that God still was busy, He has not wound up this world like a clock and left it. Mind you, they understood Him to claim the power of God and He did not deny it but affirmed it. Not to honor Christ is not to honor God as He plainly stated in verse 23. Men who boast of being deists but not Christians should read carefully. To hear the Word and believe God is to have eternal life. It is the same as receiving Christ in John 3:36.

Our Lord sets forth two resurrections. First, the spiritual resurrection of those dead in trespasses and sins, "the hour is coming and now is." Then, the future godly resurrection when all that are in the graves shall hear His voice and come forth, the good to life and the wicked to damnation. The resurrection of the righteous is the first resurrection and corresponds with the raptures of the church (1 Cor. 15:51-53; 1 Thess. 4:13-18.)

Jesus declares that of Himself He can do nothing. Now that ought to humble the rest of us! Then He sets forth four witnesses of His work; John the Baptist was the first witness (32-34). Then, our Lord's own works testify that He came from God for no man could do such miracles except God were with him (John 3:2). The Father Himself bore witness by His voice from Heaven at His Son's baptism. And the Scriptures testified of Him but while Jews searched the Scriptures they would not come to Christ and live.

There is an idea going the rounds that the Scriptures alone are sufficient, that one needs only to give forth the Word as though that were the whole matter. But many receive the seed on ground that does not yield harvest. The parable of the sower makes this clear. The Word must be mixed with faith in them that hear it (Heb. 4:2.) No one searched the Scriptures more than the pious Jew but he would not come to Christ. The Spirit must convict and the hearer must come to the Christ of Whom the Word testifies.

Our Lord concludes this discourse with a word of judgement upon Israel. They had not received Him but would receive false Christs which they have done and will do until Anti-Christ come who shall deceive them. They are condemned by Moses himself for if they had believed Moses they would have believed Him since Moses in type and figure wrote of Christ. "If you do not believe the words of Moses as they are fulfilled in me, how shall you believe my words?"

"Wilt Thou Be Made Whole?"
August 29, 1937

The fifth chapter of John records the healing of the lame man at the pool of Bethesda. Our Lord went up to Jerusalem to the feast. He attended worship and the services of God's house in His day. And He is found at the pool where the sick and afflicted gather. Human need always touched His heart. The world still gathers around its pools, and some of the waters of earth do wonderful things indeed, but beside them all stands the Christ Who alone can make us whole.

Jesus found this poor man who had been infirm for thirty-eight years. He addressed himself to this desperate case for it is usually only the desperate man who will cast himself wholly on Christ. "Wilt thou be made whole?" He asks. Today, men seek and get partial help here and there but men need to be made whole and only the Lord can perform so full a work as that. Peter said to Aeneas, "Jesus Christ maketh thee whole." His is a perfect work.

But notice this poor man's reply "Sir, I have no man...to put me in the pool." Ye see, he was looking to men. He was depending upon what men could do for him. Today do we not say, "I have no money; I have no friends; I have to 'pull'". We look to the pool and to men when there stands Jesus asking, "Wilt though be made whole?" All we need is Jesus!

And how we send people away as the disciples wanted to send the hungry multitude in Matthew 14 when Jesus replied, "They need not depart; give ye them to eat." We let men go away to seek help here and yonder when Christ alone can meet their need. If we claim to have the Gospel we ought to feed them. There is everything in Christ that men need, yet the church lets men go to the world and to fads and isms for help.

The Lord commanded the man to rise, take up his bed and walk. It seems a strange command; was not that the very thing he could not do? But the minute he made the effort in faith and at Christ's command, the power was supplied and the miracle was done. There is a split-second of obedience that makes the difference between having your back on the bed and your bed on your back. If Christ commands the impossible and we by faith make the effort to do the impossible believing in Him, it shall be done. The power is supplied the moment we make the move of faith in His Name.

Of course the Pharisees objected. They asked, "What man is that which said unto thee, Take up thy bed and walk?" They did not credit His deity. Nor did they recognize the miracle for they did not ask, "Who healed you?" but "Who said?" Later, the Lord finds the man in one temple. The place to be found after God heals you is in God's house. You will meet Christ in the church and improve your acquaintance with Him there. Our Lord warns him to sin no more, lest a worse thing befall him. Those who continue in sin may expect worse and worse rewards.

Are you at the pool? Look not at it or to the help of men. Jesus can work a perfect miracle. Wilt thou be made whole?

"I Am the Life"
March 11, 1934

In our last article we spoke of how men look everywhere for life and few find it. It is possible for one to search the Scriptures and not know the life presented there. The reason is stated by our Lord: "(Ye) search the Scriptures for in them ye think ye have eternal life: and they are they which testify of me. And ye will not come to me, that ye might have life" (John 5:39, 40).

The true and eternal life which is the only worthwhile ideal of life is not found a philosophy nor a principle but in a Person, the Lord Jesus Christ. He expressly declared: "I am the way, the truth and the life: no man cometh unto the Father, but by me" (John 14:6). God is the One Source of life and Christ is the only way to God. He further declared: "And this is life eternal, that they might know thee the only true God, and Jesus Christ, whom thou has sent" (John 17:3). He came that we might have life and that we might have it more abundantly (John 10:10). The book of John was written that, believing in Christ, we might have life through His Name (John 20:31).

This means far more than that Jesus Christ preached eternal life or gave a philosophy or even lived it. It means that the very life of God, not that physical existence which we all share, but the eternal life by which God lives was incarnate in Christ and through Him is communicable to us.

"In Him was life and the life was the light of men" (John 1:4). If He were only a teacher of life we should still be in our hopeless condition. But He embodied the life He taught and we through faith in Him can share it.

Even this is not enough, that He was that life incarnate, the Word made flesh, God with us. It was necessary for Him to die as a man that His life might be available to all men. In the twelfth chapter of John He emphasizes that. Certain Greeks had come to see Him, doubtless men of a philosophical mind, who hoped to find in His teaching an "open sesame" to truth and life but the Lord Jesus, when notified of their presence, began at once to speak of His approaching death (v. 23-33). Here lies a profound truth. Sin has cursed the human race and sin hinders men from knowing life so that the natural man cannot receive life or the truth about it. But the Lord Jesus Christ met the problem of sin for us although He knew no sin. Not that He rose from the dead and the Spirit has been sent the benefits of His life and death are available to all men. As Moses lifted up the serpent that men might have life for a look even so was Christ lifted that whosoever believeth in Him might not perish but have eternal life (John 3:14-16).

Of course, such a truth involves great mysteries. It is the fashion of the times to sneer at the idea that any one person has ever known, to say nothing of his having been, the secret of life eternal. So men still chase speculations and vain philosophies. And they will not come unto Him that they might have life.

Col. 3:4 calls Christ "our life." When we believe in Him and yield ourselves to Him God gives us a new and eternal life which is His own shared with us. It is not merely that we set out to live like Jesus: He becomes our very life so that we can say "to me to live is Christ," not simply "like Christ" nor "for Christ"; He is life itself. We are "partakers of the divine nature" (2 Pt. 1:4) and therefore of the divine life.

"At the Feast"
January 5, 1936

The seventh chapter of John records our Lord's experience at the feast of tabernacles. His brothers, looking at things from an ordinary, business-like standpoint, urged Him to go up to Judea and get Himself before the people. His answer is striking, "My time is not yet come: but your time is always ready." Jesus lived in God's will and awaited His time. Men have no "time," they follow their own impulses.

But our Lord did go up to the feast as it were in secret. He did not court persecution even as He advised His disciples to flee from it. At the feast He created much discussion especially among those who thought one could not teach if he had not had the regular training. (Their number still is legion!) He answers that His doctrine is of God and that willingness to do God's will is the key to spiritual knowledge. Decision leads to precision. Obedience is the path to certainty. They condemned Him for healing on the Sabbath, the healing of the impotent man over a year before, but He replies that they circumcise on the Sabbath, yet censure Him for healing. They were confused as to how Messiah should come but He replies that soon He will leave them and they will seek and not find Him.

Verses 37 to 39 contain our Lord's great invitation to the thirsty to drink from Him the Living Water of the Spirit.

Here we have the five-fold secret of the filling of the Spirit, thirsting, coming, drinking, believing, overflowing. Notice that our Lord keeps the center of the stage, "Let Him come unto me," "He that believeth on Me," "they that believe on Him." The work of the spirit is to testify to Him, the Spirit must never become the figure-head of any movement.

There is a hidden truth in verse 39 that the Spirit was not yet given because Jesus was not yet glorified. It is also true in experience that the Spirit is not given to us in fulness, until Jesus is glorified in our lives. Pentecost must always follow ascension.

Such mighty teaching produces great confusion among the people, some saying one thing and some another. There is something almost comical in the vanity of the Pharisees when they proudly ask, "Have any of the rulers or of the Pharisees believed on Him?" As if that settled it! "But this people who knoweth not the law are cursed." Could conceit be any more stupid than that! How true that He came that those who saw should be blinded and that the blind should see!

Nicodemus interposes a word in our Lord's behalf. But it is a lame defense and brings a fierce rejoined: "Art thou also of Galilee? Search and look: for out of Galilee ariseth no prophet." But Jonah and Elijah both came from Galilee. Truly, they are "blind leaders of the blind." Poor scribes, looking for a Messiah of place rather than of power. They did err, not knowing the Scriptures nor the power of God.

"Go and Sin No More"
January 12, 1936

Only John records the story of the woman taken in adultery (8:1-11). The story is not found in some of the oldest manuscripts and Augustine says it was left out of many copies for fear it might teach immorality!

It seems to have been a scheme of the crafty scribes and Pharisees to cause Jesus to pronounce upon a matter which really belonged to the legal and civil authorities. But the Lord merely wrote upon the ground, a way of signifying unwillingness to deal with the matter in hand. It would be well if we learned to write in the sand and say nothing when many matters come up into which we need not be drawn. When reputations are attacked and personalities are involved and we are asked to pass judgment upon others, let us write in the sand, as though we heard them not. We are not appointed to be judge and divider and we shall save ourselves much trouble if we learn the art of writing in the sand.

But the accusers press for an answer. They are sure they have trapped the Lord. If He condemns the woman, they will say He has taken undue authority to judge in legal matters. If He does not condemn her, they will say He makes for loose morals and laxity of the law. Then He turns the tables upon them and they are taken in their own snare: "Let him that is without sin cast the first stone. He neither justifies her conduct nor does He condemn her, yet He completely defeats the accusers. Since there was no one present except Himself who possessed that qualification the accusers slink away leaving only the sinless One and the sinful one. The only one who had a right to cast the first stone has rather mercy and love.

Wonderful is His word to the woman, "Neither do I condemn thee: go, and sin no more." He did not excuse nor justify her sin but He only said He was not passing judgment upon her. We must remember that one day He is to be judge and we are to be judged according to the deeds done in the body. This passage need not make for any light attitude toward our Lord's position as to sin. He simply was declaring here His unwillingness to exercise the civil and legal authority of His time.

Likely, the woman had repented and our Lord knew it. He seems to include in not condemning her His gracious forgiveness. How blessed to know that, though we have sinned, we may go and sin no more!

Throughout the whole story runs the precious note of compassion for the weak and erring. Too easily do we sit in judgment and forget that we also are not without sin. Writing on the ground will become us far better than casting stones. To be sure, there arise occasions when, as with Paul and the offending brother in Corinth, believers must take action in church discipline but it is not for us to sentence sinners but to seek to bring them to forgiveness through faith in Him who, though now their Saviour and our Advocate, will one day be Judge.

"Let Your Light So Shine"
December 10, 1933

In John 8:12 our Lord says, "I am the light of the world," He was "the true Light which lighteth eery man that cometh into the world" (John 1:9). "I am come a light into the world," he declared in John 12:46. In the New Jerusalem "the Lamb is the light thereof" (Rev. 21:22).

In Mt. 5:74 Jesus says to His disciples, "Ye are the light of the world." "He that followeth me shall not walk in darkness, but shall have the light of life", He tells us in John 8:12 and this Light shines forth from our hearts, the Light of the Indwelling Christ, so that we shine as lights in the world (Phil. 2:15.) The Light is not generated within us by our own efforts; we are not the sources but simply the instruments in and from which the Light shines. The Light is Christ living within because we have believed in Him and have been born again.

Jesus went on to say, "A city that is set on a hill cannot be hid." We are higher than the world and nothing can hide the influence of a life that is in the will of God. Trouble and temptation and persecution only fan the flame. The life that is hid with Christ in God cannot be hidden in its outward influence for God.

Our Lord then gives us further teaching about our light-bearing. He states the negative side first. "Neither do men light a candle, and put it under a bushel, but on a candlestick; and it giveth light unto all that are in the house." Indifference and worldliness, neglect of duty and any disobedience of the law of Christ, these are bushels that quench the Spirit and spoil our influence. Candles are meant for candlesticks. Our influence will take care of itself if we are in the candlestick of His will.

Then, Jesus gives us positive instruction. "Let your light so shine before men, that they may see your good works, and glorify your Father which is in heaven." Mind you, He does not say "Shine your light" but "Let it shine." Some believers are much concerned about their influence. They strain and strive trying to make good impressions and labour that others may see how good they are. They are shining their light. But we need only to abide in Him, beware of all "bushels," and the light will shine of its own accord.

We are to let our light shine before men. We are not to hide in a cave but live His life right out in the world of things as they are. The real saint is no cloistered recluse but one who can meet life's wear and tear through Christ. We are to let our light so shine before men that they may see our good works. Not just in order that they may see our good works and nothing more, to be sure, but they must see our good works if they are to be influenced. Men cannot see inside our hearts and tell what sort of faith we have; they can see only our works. We are His workmanship, created in Christ Jesus unto good works (Eph. 2:10) and faith without works is dead (Jas. 2:20.)

The purpose of it all is they may glorify not us, but our Father in heaven. "Whatsoever ye do, do all to the glory of God" (1 Cor. 10:31.) That is the secret of unselfish goodness, living solely that God may be glorified. It is easy to take pride in our own influence for Christ so that He decreases and we increase. We must ever remember to be only the friend of the bridegroom.

"The Light of the World"
January 19, 1936

After the touching incident of the woman taken in adultery John records our Lord's discourse on light and freedom (8:12-59). Our Lord declares Himself to be the light of the world. We who believe are also the light of the world (Mt. 5:14) but our light is the reflected light of Christ.

In John's great passage Jesus offers the double witness of Himself and the Father (verse 18.) He tells the Pharisees they will die in their sins (verse 21) because they do not believe in Him (24.) We are condemned already, (John 3:18), we are under the wrath of God (John 3:36), and we shall die in our sins if we believe Him not. It is not drunkenness or immorality but simplistic unbelief that sends men to hell.

Again and again in this chapter (verses 24, 25, 28) Jesus makes the claim to be the Christ. The truly ideal life is salted in verse 29; "And He that sent me is with me; the Father hath not left me alone; for I do always those things that please Him." Companionship and conformity! But He follows this statement with, "if ye continue in my word, then are ye my disciples indeed; and ye shall know the truth and the truth shall make you free" following it in verse 36 with "If the Son shall make you free, ye shall be free indeed." Some had believed on account of His words in verse 29 but He made it clear that first contact must be followed by continuance. Looking into the law of liberty must be followed by continuing therein (Jas. 1:25).

The Pharisees prided themselves upon their Abrahamic descent but our Lord calls them children of the devil (verse 41). Advocates of the modern "fatherhood of God" idea would do well to ponder this verse. Here were Jews of God's favored race claiming "one Father, even God" (verse 41) but our Lord speedily smashes that claim with His flaming answer. Soft preaching today stands in need of revision according to John 8.

Follows a clear claim to sinlessness which no man could dare to make (verse 46.) Again He tells them they are not of God and follows with His staggering claim that those who keep His sayings shall never see death. The opposition grows more bitter with every exchange of words. They reply that even Abraham died and yet He claims to be greater than Abraham. This leads to the climax when our Lord declares, "Before Abraham was, I am." Here is one of the most stupendous claims of the Christ in the four gospels. Notice, He does not say, "Before Abraham was, I was." He links Himself with the Eternal I Am That I Am of the Old Testament.

It is no wonder that the Pharisees tried to kill Him. Here were the religious people of that day, strict in observing the law, proud of Abraham and Moses, being told that they were children of the devil and that One stood among them greater than Abraham, living before Abraham, and that Abraham saw Christ's day by faith and was glad. One wonders what He would say today if He were among us with audible voice for Pharisaism is still with us. Would not men who pride themselves upon the Fatherhood of God be called again the children of the devil?

"The Good Shepherd"
February 2, 1936

Our Lord's discourse about Himself as the Good Shepherd has been a favorite portion of the Word through the ages. Here (John 10:1-21) He declares that only those spiritual leaders who come in by the Door which is Himself are authorized to lead the sheep. He speaks first of under-shepherds. The church is the sheep-fold, believers are the sheep.

He then declares Himself to be the Door. Those who enter in by Him are saved, thus setting forth the certainty of the Gospel. They shall go in and out, signifying the liberty of the Gospel. They shall find pasture, showing the satisfaction of the Gospel.

All false prophets who came before Jesus He declares to be thieves and robbers who came to kill and destroy. He came that men might have life and not a narrowed and restricted life but life more abundantly, life rich and full and plentiful and overflowing.

Then the Lord passes on to another figure and speaks of Himself as the Good Shepherd Who laid down His life for the sheep. He knows His own,–and what a strengthening thought is that! His own know Him. He also declared that He had other sheep not of this fold, meaning the Gentiles who are to be and now are brought into the fold through

Him Who broke down the middle wall of partition.

Our Lord's statement, "Therefore doth my Father love me, because I lay down my life, that I might take it again" contains a claim which no mere man ever could make. It declares the voluntariness of our Lord's death and also the stupendous fact that He could take up His life again which He did at the resurrection. However, this laying down His life and taking it up again was by the commandment of God so that, although the power was His, He died and rose in obedience and that He was always subject to God. If He must obey how much more must we! We try to substitute many things for obedience and devise numberless detours to dodge the practical keeping of His commandments. Many Christians consecrate and dedicate and pray for blessings and waste years seeking strange experiences when they will not take the next step of doing what the Lord commands.

Enter in at the door for there is no other entrance and no man cometh to the Father but by Him. Let Him be your shepherd for all others lead into the wilderness and lose you. And remember that He leaves the ninety and nine to seek the one that is lost that He might bear it back to the fold rejoicing.

"Christ the Door"
August 1, 1937

"I am the door: by me if any man enter in, he shall be saved, and shall go in and out, and find pasture."
Our Lord is the Door, the Door to the Fold of God's Elect, to the Church. He is the Way to God, the Truth, the Life, He is the Door to all that is of God for in Him dwells all the fulness of the God-head bodily. There is no other entrance and He alone has the right to say, "I am the Door."
"By me," "No man cometh to the Father but by Me."
The world has its philosophies, its modern gospels, its syncretisms of many faiths but the only Gospel that is the power of God unto salvation is the Gospel of no other Name. He is not merely one of the doors. The world wants us to be "broadminded" but strait is the gate and narrow is the way that leads to life. He who climbs over any other way is a thief and a robber.
"If any man enter in." Thank God for the universality of the Gospel: "Whosoever will may come." Don't freeze up on predestination. It is all right to talk predestination to Christians who are already among the elect but to the sinner say, "Repent and be baptized, every one of you in the name of Jesus Christ."
"He shall be saved." Not "maybe" or "probably," but "he shall be saved." Don't say you have a "hope." If you are in

Him you have a certainty. You don't just hope that you are married; you either know that you are or you aren't and your salvation ought to be as definite.

"And shall go in and out." The liberty of a Christian! If the Son makes us free we are free indeed. The world thinks of us as restricted and bound but we are fee to do all that is good. We are freed from sin and from the world and from doubt and from fear. We have not the spirit of bondage again to fear but the spirit of adoption whereby we cry "Abba, Father." But we are free as we continue in the Word. A true disciple is one who grows and follows the Lord from one grade to another. We can become perfect for that grade but there are always more grades ahead. And we are to continue both to read and to heed the Word for if we know these things, happy are we if we do them.

"And shall find pasture." Sin fills but it does not satisfy. The Lord fills our mouths with good things. If we are willing and obedient, we shall eat of the good of the land. Some are dyspeptic and won't eat or exercise. Others are fed up on the devil's sweetmeats and have no appetite. Christ is the Door to the promised land of a satisfying Christian life and it is a land flowing with milk and honey, the figs and pomegranates and grapes of Eschol. It is not necessary to leave Canaan for any satisfaction outside. If we trust in the Lord and do good we shall dwell in the land and be fed. All else is sawdust and shavings.

He is the Door. There is no other way. Any one may enter and to enter is to be saved.

"The Raising of Lazarus"
May 10, 1936

After the raising of Lazarus, the enemies of Jesus at once went into a huddle (John 11:46-57). The devil's crowd gets busy when God's power begins to be manifested mightily. Caiaphas, the high priest, spoke more than he knew, the inspiration of old being restored for the moment. God thus caused one of Jesus' bitterest enemies to proclaim the atonement and the gathering of Israel in Christ! How God does make even the wrath of men to praise Him!

On His way to Jerusalem our Lord was met by 10 lepers beseeching Him for mercy. He simply told them to go show themselves to the priests as cleansed persons and we read that "as they went, they were cleansed." What a lesson in faith! They could have said, "What! Go to the priests as though we are healed! We are not going to witness to what we don't have!" But faith simply took Jesus at His Word and as they walked by faith, the wonder was wrought. We demand that we see before we believe. Faith steps out, looking no better and feeling no better, but believing that He is faithful Who promised. As we go we are cleansed.

Only one of the 10 returned to give thanks but he was rewarded by being made whole, not only in body but entirely. The entire story (Lk. 17:11-19) set forth the blessing of God when we simply obey like Naaman who went to wash in the Jordan though he felt no better and it looked like a fool's errand.

The Pharisees demand to know when the kingdom of God shall come. Jesus replies that the kingdom is in the midst of them. He did not mean that it was within those self-righteous Pharisees but that in Himself the kingdom was among them but they refused it. During the present church-age the Kingdom is a spiritual matter and not outward but when the Lord returns to reign it will be an outward matter, visible to all. The Bible speaks of that day and says it will be as it was in the days of Noah. We are living in such a time now. Men are eating and drinking and marrying wives and buying and selling and planting and building. They are indifferent to the Lord's return and even professing Christians ask, "Where are the signs of His coming?"

But He will come. Many, like Lot's wife will be looking back upon the city of Sodom. There may be a reference here first of all to the fall of Jerusalem but that was a type of the Lord's return. Our Lord's strange statement: "Wheresoever the body is, there will the eagles be gathered together" has its primary application in the Roman soldiers who wrought God's vengeance upon Jerusalem but broadly it means, "Wherever there is sin and national putrefaction, there will the avenging forces fall in judgment." This will reach its climax at Armageddon, the last great battle.

"The Farewell Discourse"
July 19, 1936

Precious to many hearts are chapters 14-17 of John's Gospel. Here our Lord on the eve of His death opens His very heart. He promises to prepare for us a place and return to receive us. He is the way, truth and life. To Philip who asks to see God, He answers "Have I been so long time with you and yet hast thou not known me?" To know Him is to know the Father. He promises to send the Paraclete Who is Another, not just the spirit of Jesus. He and the Father will manifest themselves to such as have and keep the comments (v.21). The way to know Jesus better is to obey Him. The Holy Spirit will be our Teacher. And in such a dark hour, our Lord bequeaths His peace!

The much-discussed parable of the vine (Chapter 15) simply illustrates union with Christ and abiding in Him. The unfruitful are removed; the fruitful pruned. His Words must abide in us, in that we read and heed them. Practical obedience is the secret of abiding. He wants our joy to be full, not partial. We are His friends if we do His will, not just because we sing or talk about Him at church. He has chosen us to bear fruit, the fruit of the Spirit (Gal. 5:22,23). We may expect to be hated by the world if we are His. The Holy Spirit testifies not of Himself but of Christ–never make the Spirit the figurehead in any movement. He but speaks of Christ.

In Chapter 16 our Lord prepares His disciples for the

adversity ahead. He must go that the Comforter might come. Jesus in the flesh could reach only a few; the Spirit is accessible to all. The Spirit convicts of sin; of righteousness by holding up Christ the perfect righteousness of judgment because in Christ Satan is judged and condemned. The Spirit will guide us into all truth. He comforts them in their sorrow by calling to mind the greater glory He will reach through His suffering. He claims all that God has for His own. In verse 33 He promises both trouble and triumph. When we are in tribulation God is keeping one promise but in giving us victory He keeps the other!

Our Lord prays His high-priestly prayer in Chapter 17. Here we see what power was our Lord's and His perfect communion with the Father. Life eternal is to know God in Christ. He has kept His great commission and has glorified God and manifested His Name and given us His Word. He prays for all believers to the Father that they may be one and be kept of God. We believe God hears this prayer and that none shall be plucked out of the Father's hand. He prays that we may be where He is, which He promised in Chapter 14. How blessed to know that He still is our Advocate (1 John 2:1) and that the Spirit prays for us! (Rom. 8:26).

From this prayer our Lord goes to the agony of Gethsemane, praying not to dodge the cross as some see it, but to be spared death before He reached the cross. The three disciples who had slept at His transfiguration glory sleep now in His agony. What a commentary on human nature, to sleep on two such momentous occasions!

At His arrest our Lord's very presence confounds His enemies (John 18:6). Impulsive Peter uses the sword which our Lord repudiates as an instrument of His kingdom. He could call legions of angels if He needed them! Through it all He moves majestically, deeply conscious that He is fulfilling Scripture, not a mere martyr but the Son of God giving Himself for the world.

"Constantly Abiding"
April 1, 1934

We live in a nervous, high-strung age. Believers live tensely and churches strain and strive to raise expenses. Those who really are concerned about the deeper Christian life often worry about it and fret trying to be Christ-like!

In such a feverish age it is refreshing to go back to the fifteenth chapter of John and read Jesus' simple discourse about the vine and the branches. He tells us that He is the Vine, His Father is the Husbandman and we are the branches. Our duty is not to strain and strive trying to stay in the Vine or to produce fruit: we are simply to abide in Him, keep the fellowship with Him unhindered, with no sin unconfessed, no interest He cannot share, leaving all life's burdens with Him, drawing from Him all wisdom, life and strength. If we thus abide we are promised certain precious things in His Word.

First, let us say that only through the new birth do we come into true relationship with Him. Others attach themselves to Him in other ways but these are taken away (John 15:2, 6). Being born again we become vitally identified with Him, "partakers of the divine nature" (2 Pt. 1:4), "members of His body, of His flesh and of His bones" (Eph. 5:30).

Our relationship is fixed but our fellowship with Him

depends upon whether we abide in Him as we ought. This abiding is not a tense and strained affair but an utter dependence upon Him for every need, feeding upon Him, drawing from Him as the branch from the vine, all strength and security. This abiding means obedience–"He that saith he abideth in Him ought himself also so to walk even as He walked" (1 John 2:6)–but our greatest obedience is to abide in Him. Abiding is revealed in holy living: "whosoever abideth in Him sinneth not" (1 John 3:6). This is not sinless perfection but living above wilful and habitual sin.

This abiding is witnessed by the Spirit: "And hereby, we know that he abideth in us by the Spirit which He hath given us" (1 John 3:24). It is perfected by purging; "every branch that beareth fruit He purgeth it that it may bring forth more fruit" (John 15:2). Some believers worry over chastening as though it were a sign of God's disfavor. But it is the productive life that God prunes and disciplines that it may be even more fruitful.

Abiding in Him is also the condition of answered prayer: "If ye abide in me, and my word abide in you, ye shall ask what ye will and it shall be done unto you" (John 15:7). This reminds us of the discourse on the Bread of Life in John 6. When the disciples complained that He was declaring a hard saying, He simplified it by saying: "The words that I speak unto you, they are spirit, and they are life." So here He makes His abiding in us clearer by saying "if my words abide in you." We are to feed upon His truth and if we do our prayers shall be answered.

This abiding is manifested in fruitfulness. "He that abideth in me, and I in him, the same bringeth forth much fruit" (John 15:5). Notice that the fruit-bearing is just the natural consequence of abiding. We fret and worry about results, our good deeds, our behavior, churches bother about by-products, when our interest should be concentrated upon this focal point, to abide in Him. That is our business; all

"Constantly Abiding"

else is a natural result.

"And now, little children, abide in Him; that, when He shall appear, we may have confidence, and not be ashamed before Him at His coming" (1 John 2:28).

The following Havner CDs are available for $12.00 each plus shipping. Contact the Sherwood Communications Group, 2201 Whispering Pines Rd., Albany, GA 31707 or www.VanceHavner.com

#1 The Country and the Church
Sparrows in the Bible

#2 Getting Used to the Dark
Home Before Dark

#3 The Budget and the Boy
Look Who's Here

#4 The Unfinished Work of Christ
Lordship of Christ

#5 As He Is So Are We
Sanctified Extravagance

#6 Knowing What To Do
Sinning Against the Light

#7 Must I Live
Is This That
The Preacher

#8 What Jesus Wants For His Church
The Wonder

#9 The Christian in this World
Old Time Religion

#10 Look Who's Here
Must I Live

#11 Forget Not All His Benefits
Begin Being Like Him

#12 What We Have Now and What Is Coming
Great Decisions of the Bible

#13 Don't Miss Your Miracle
O Glorious Day

#14 From Groans to Glory
Survival of Christianity

Printed in the United States
1038000003B/58-1008